2nd Edition

THE BASICS
VOLUME 1

By David A. Lien

COMPUSOFT® PUBLISHING

Contents

Acknowledgments

Project Coordinator:
Jackie Bohan

Editorial Director
Inez Goldberg

Production Coordinator
Janice Scanlan

Technical Editors
Inez Goldberg
Jody Bailey
Dan Gookin

Cover and Book Design
Masar/Johnston Advertising and Design

Composition Design:
Gary Williams

Illustrations:
Martin Lindsay
Bob Stevens

Printer:
Arcata Graphics/Fairfield

INTRODUCTION

What Is MS-DOS and What Does It Do?

Before we get into MS-DOS, the **M**icrosoft **D**isk **O**perating System, and what it can do, let's take a brief look at what makes the computer itself tick. Don't get nervous; this isn't going to be a technical treatise. Computers are actually pretty simple underneath all the bells and whistles. At least, they operate on a fairly simple principle. Take a few minutes to read this introduction. It may answer some of your preliminary questions and satisfy your curiosity. You'll have your fingers on the keyboard in no time.

How a Computer Works (More or Less)

You may have heard the expression, "A computer without software is completely dumb." For all practical purposes, that is a true statement. Software is usually thought of as packaged programs with specific tasks, like the SCRIPSIT word processor or the Multiplan spreadsheet, but in fact, software is any information put into the computer. It may be "loaded" from a diskette or typed in at the keyboard, or it may even be permanently "burned" into the computer's memory chips.

A computer is essentially a passive device. It has lots of potential and is able to go to work when told to do so, but it has no "brains" of its own.

It has to be told, for example, to put the cursor on the screen and where to put it. (The cursor is the small flashing light on the screen that indicates where the next character will appear.) It has to be told to make the disks spin and what copyright notice to put on the screen when you first turn it on. In short, it has to be told everything.

First, There's ROM

Some of the information the computer needs just to get up in the morning is permanently embedded in a special place in the internal circuitry called ROM. ROM is *Read-Only Memory*, which simply means that the computer can only *read* the *memory*; it can't change it in any way. How can information be stored permanently in an electronic device that is turned off? Here's a gross over-simplification:

Turn the Computer On

You've probably already done this, but if not (and if they are separate pieces), be sure the monitor and keyboard are plugged into the computer and that the power cords are all plugged in. Don't worry about putting any disks in the drives yet, just turn on the computer and monitor. In a moment, a copyright notice will appear on the screen.

Move up close to the screen and look at the individual letters. Notice how they are made up of tiny dots? Each one of those dots is lit up because a certain electronic "switch" is turned on inside the computer. Believe it or not, as complicated and powerful as computers can be, they really only understand two things: *on* and *off*. The most awesome software program on the market-- one that would make the computer draw the Mona Lisa or dance a jig--is nothing more than a long list of on/off instructions. On or off, yes or no, one or zero--in the final analysis, that's really all there is to it.

The memory circuits contain millions of "switches," and software turns them on and off in a very precise order. So, how can the computer do things like putting the copyright notice on the screen without software to flip its switches? Simple; the specific switches required for this job are "welded" in the *on* position at the factory.

As little information as possible is stored in the permanent ROM. There are two reasons: First, the designers want to keep the computer flexible so it can be "programmed" later with a maximum of freedom, and second, the memory area needs to be kept free for *your* data.

Along Comes MS-DOS

Considerable "housekeeping," or management, is required to keep the computer running efficiently. Remember, the computer itself, though teeming with potential, is pretty ignorant, and that's where MS-DOS, the *Disk Operating System,* comes in. The information in ROM keeps the computer organized enough to accept and to "understand" what MS-DOS tells it. When loaded from disk into the computer, MS-DOS becomes the director and manages the many activities going on at the same time.

MS-DOS is itself a program written in a "language" that the computer understands and is able to obey. It sends out the instructions for loading and running software programs, for directing data from the keyboard and disks to the screen or printer, and for the host of other functions needed so the computer can do more than display its own copyright data.

Then There's Application Software

The system management capabilities of MS-DOS remain in the computer's memory even if you remove the MS-DOS disk and load in another program. (If you have a software program that doesn't require you to "boot up" with MS-DOS first, then that software contains the appropriate parts of MS-DOS.) DOS is necessary, and it must be present, one way or another.

But MS-DOS does more than simply keep everything flowing smoothly. When you create documents or other *files* with your application software, they can be recorded, or *saved*, onto disk. MS-DOS permits you to move those files around, to make copies of them from disk to disk, to delete them, to connect one to another, and so on. It also prepares diskettes to work on your particular computer and to make copies of those disks for safekeeping or for giving to other operators.

Included on the MS-DOS disk are many other special-purpose programs including BASIC, the most popular computer language for creating your own programs, and Edlin, an easy-to-use editor for writing and editing text files. We will learn how to use the more important ones soon.

What It Means to Be "In" MS-DOS

MS-DOS is always working in the background, making sure, for example, that when the ⌷M⌷ key is pressed, an M appears on the screen. But how do we tell it to do the many other promised tricks?

When you first start up the computer (in Chapter 1), you'll insert the MS-DOS disk and type in the date and time. Once that's done, a *prompt* will appear on the screen that looks like this:

A>

That prompt means that MS-DOS is ready and at your service. It indicates that the computer is at what is called the *command* level. Want to make MS-DOS do tricks? Give it commands. That's how it works. The two volumes in this series tell you what all the commands are and explain how to use them.

Once you load a commercial software program, like DeskMate, the MS-DOS A> prompt goes away. This means that while the DOS system management will still be taken care of, the MS-DOS file and disk handling features are no longer available. To use them, you must return to the MS-DOS command level and to the A> prompt.

The Three Parts of MS-DOS

I. The job of actually *operating* the system is handled by a part called, appropriately, the *System*. You can forget about this part of MS-DOS. The commands and instructions in the System are strictly between MS-DOS and the computer and neither require nor permit participation by the operator. Once the MS-DOS disk has been put into the computer and you've entered the date and time, the A> prompt appears and the System is loaded into the computer's memory. At this point, you could remove the MS-DOS disk and put it in the closet and close the door if you want. The *System* will stay in the computer until you turn the power off or press the Reset button.

II. Once the date and time have been entered, some of the simpler MS-DOS functions are also loaded into the computer's memory. Commands to do things like copy and delete files are available even when the MS-DOS disk has been removed. These commands are called *internal* commands because the instructions they require are loaded into the computer's internal memory. All you have to remember about internal commands is that, once loaded at startup time, the MS-DOS disk need not be present to use them. They stay in the computer until it is shut off or reset.

III. More complicated DOS programs, like the Edlin editor and the BASIC programming language, take up too much valuable memory to keep inside the computer at all times, so they are kept on the disk and are loaded in only when needed. Predictably, the commands that call up these larger programs are called *external* commands. Remember that external commands require the MS-DOS disk to be in the disk drive.

This book explains the most important commands and teaches you how to do the things you'll need for day-to-day use of your computer. (Volume 2 teaches you the rest.) From here on, you'll learn by doing.

Have fun! You have a lot of power at your command.

P A R T   1

Startup to shutdown

CHAPTER 1

Starting up the System

This book applies to all the Tandy MS-DOS computers, each of which is slightly different from the others. To avoid unnecessary repetition of the obvious, we have selected the Tandy 1000 as the "standard" and written specifically to it.

Furthermore, we have assumed that you have a Tandy 1000 with 128K of memory, two floppy disk drives, MS-DOS version 2.11, a monochrome monitor, and possibly, a printer.

For convenience, reference is sometimes made to the "1000 Series" (i.e., Tandy 1000, 1000 EX, and 1000 SX) or "3000 Series" (i.e., Tandy 3000 and 3000 HL) because of the similarity of keyboards and drive location. Other times reference is made to the "2.11 Series" or "3.2 Series" referring to the computers using those versions of MS-DOS.

Don't worry if your computer is equipped differently or if you have a different model. Those few really significant differences are flagged where appropriate. The remaining differences (such as the location of the keys on the keyboard and the appearance of the cursor) are so slight and obvious that you will have no trouble adjusting to them. This book was tested on every model available at the time of publication.

Tandy 3000 Series users, read Appendix A first.

3

Startup

Double-check that everything is hooked up properly, then turn on the printer and, if you have one, the external hard drive. Finally, turn on your computer and then the monitor.

Next, put the MS-DOS disk, label up, in Drive A (the top drive in the 3000 Series; the bottom drive in the other computers), and close the drive door latch. If nothing happens, or if you see only a "Memory Size" or error message, press the Reset button (or the [Ctrl] [Alt] and [Del] keys at the same time).

A faster, more convenient way to do all this is to invest in a power strip and plug everything--your computer and all its peripheral devices--into it. Make it a habit to leave everything turned on and simply use the main switch on the strip for startup and shutdown. Just remember to put the MS-DOS disk in the drive *after* you turned everything on and to remove it *before* you turn everything off. More on this later.

After some copyright information, this message appears:

```
Command v. 2.11
Current date is Tue  1-01-1980
Enter new date:
```

(Remember, the Tandy 1000 is the "reference." The 3.2 Series will not display the command version line.)

Setting the date is usually a good idea (so we will), but should you decide not to bother with it in the future, pressing [ENTER] here will bypass date-setting and move on to time-setting. The time can also be bypassed with [ENTER] if desired. (Users with an internal clock option should refer to their clock's manual for instructions on setting up the internal clock.)

Tandy 3000 Series users can ignore the next two sections. Once the 3000's internal clock has been set (either by a Tandy technician or with the special SETUP program), there is no need to enter a new time and date. Simply press [ENTER] at these two prompts.

Setting the Date

Type in today's date. A leading zero is not required for single-digit months or days, and the year can be typed in with either the last two or all four digits. Use hyphens, slashes or periods to separate them. No need to put in the day of the week; MS-DOS will calculate that, taking into account everything including leap years. The simplest format for a date of January 1, 1987 is probably:

1.1.87 [ENTER]

This is simplest because it takes advantage of the numeric keypad located on the right side of the keyboard. Notice that this calculator-style "ten-key" pad includes a period key and an [ENTER] key making the entering of dates a quick, one-hand operation. To use the numeric keypad, press the [NUM LOCK] key. A small light will come on when the key's locked, and the keypad will produce numbers. Press the key again to unlock.

Setting the Time

There are occasions, particularly when using application programs, when it's useful for the computer to record the correct time. The ten-key pad can be used to set the time as well:

10.25.55 [ENTER]

The clock starts when the [ENTER] key is pressed, so if accuracy is important, set the time a few seconds from now, then press the [ENTER] key when that precise moment arrives. AM and PM are handled by using 24-hour time; use 13 for 1 PM, 14 for 2 PM, etc. Should you make any mistakes in entering the date or time, use the [←] or [BACKSPACE] key to back up. (3000 Series users, the backspace key is labeled [←]. You can't use the [←] (left arrow key) when the [Num Lock] key is on.) Either key will erase characters as the cursor moves back over them. Then type the correct ones. Once date and time are set, the *MS-DOS* clock keeps running until the computer is turned off. An *internal* clock is powered by a separate battery and keeps correct time whether the computer is on or off. Be sure you distinguish between these two separate clocks.

The System Prompt

Pressing [ENTER] after the date and time are set brings up the *SYSTEM PROMPT*. This marker:

A>

...indicates the computer is ready to go.

To display the date, type **date** [ENTER] when the system prompt appears. Notice that an opportunity to change the MS-DOS date again is offered. If there is no need to change the date, just press [ENTER]. Time works the same way; type **time** [ENTER] to see the current time, right down to 1/100 of a second! Type in a new time or press [ENTER] to retain the time displayed.

SUMMARY

* Turn on the printer and optional hard drive first, then the computer. Insert the MS-DOS disk in Drive A.
* Press [NUM LOCK] to activate the numeric key pad. Use it to set the date and time.
* The system prompt, A>, indicates that MS-DOS is ready to go to work.
* Type **date** or **time** anytime to check the date or time.

CHAPTER 2

The Directory

Entering Commands

You may not realize it, but you just gave MS-DOS two commands. When you typed **date** and **time** at the system prompt, you told the computer to do something. Without MS-DOS to tell it how, the computer would have just sat there. A computer without an operating system is pretty helpless. The words date and time mean nothing to the computer itself, but MS-DOS knows that they mean you want to reset its clock, calculate the day of the week, display the appropriate messages and so on. Asking for the date and time gets right to the heart of what MS-DOS does--giving commands to the computer to tell it what to do and how to do it. Just about all your interaction with MS-DOS from now on will involve commands.

The Directory

Let's issue MS-DOS another command; this time type **dir** ⌑ENTER⌑. A long list scrolls up the screen. The list is, in fact, so long that you can't read the first entries before they disappear off the screen. Because it is so long, the list will have to be displayed a "page" at a time. Type the **dir** command again; this time with a short addition that says, "Give it to me a page at a time":

dir/p ⌑ENTER⌑

There, the first "page" (screenful) of this list is holding still on the screen. Only the title scrolled off, and it said:

```
Volume in drive A has no label
Directory of A:\
```

The list is a *directory*--a table of contents--of Drive A. It is a list of all the *files* on the disk in that drive. Since the MS-DOS disk is the diskette currently in Drive A, the directory on the screen is displaying the names of all the programs which make up MS-DOS. Let's take a look at it.

The Directory of the MS-DOS Disk

Volume (meaning the disk) in drive A (the disk drive) has no label (name). All this means is that no specific name has been given to this disk. Later, when you start creating, or formatting, your own disks, you'll assign them names. For now, it's nothing to worry about.

The first few entries will look something like this:*

```
COMMAND COM    15957  10-20-84    1:00P
ANSI    SYS     4399  10-20-84    1:00P
CHKDSK  COM     6468  10-20-84    1:00P
DEBUG   COM    12223  10-20-84    1:00P
```

Think of a computer disk as a bookshelf. Collectively, the shelf contains a huge amount of information, but the information is broken down into manageable pieces called books. There are skinny ones, fat ones, technical ones, non-technical ones, and some just for fun. The same applies to the diskette. Each "book," or body of information, on a disk is called a file, and the names of all the files on this particular disk are listed in the first column of the directory on the screen. COMMAND, ANSI, CHKDSK and so on are all file names. In Volume Two of this MS-DOS series, you will learn what all of these files are used for.

---

* Dates, times and sizes (the number to the left of the date) in directories will vary, depending on which computer you are using and which version of MS-DOS.

The second column tells what *kind* of a file each is, and the third column lists the size of the file in "bytes." You've probably heard a lot about bytes and kilobytes and megabytes, but in case you aren't sure what they are, here's a quick simplification: a byte is a character--a letter, number, punctuation mark or space. If a file is 15957 bytes long, it takes up the equivalent of 15957 characters (roughly 2650 six-letter words) on the disk. A Tandy 1000 or 1200 floppy disk can hold approximately 360,000 bytes. Tandy 3000 diskettes hold 1.2 megabytes. Tandy hard drives hold from 5 to 70 million bytes, or characters. (A kilobyte is a thousand bytes, and a megabyte is a million bytes).

The last two columns tell when (date and time) each file was recorded ("saved") on the disk. Once you begin to put files on your own disks, knowing when each was saved may become important.

At the bottom of the screen, there is a message:

```
Strike a key when ready . . .
```

If you've seen enough of this part of the MS-DOS directory, press the space bar or any number or letter key and the rest will scroll up. The message at the bottom of the screen tells the total number of files on this disk and the number of bytes of empty space left (may vary for different versions of MS-DOS):

```
       32 File(s)        39936 bytes free
```

You can obtain a directory of any disk you put into the computer, not just the MS-DOS disk. If you have more than one disk drive or a hard drive, you can see the directory of the disk in any drive by simply specifying the name of the drive. (We'll do that later, when you have something there to check.) The files on any drive can be subgrouped at your discretion, so that, for example, all your accounting files are in one group and all your word processing files are in another. Each group can have its own "sub-directory," and "sub-sub-directories." This *Tree Structuring* of files is covered in detail in Volume Two.

For the time being, it's only necessary to be able to see what's on a given disk. As a matter of fact, the directory already gives you more information than you probably want to know. There really ought to be a way to display a list of only the names of the files on a disk, without all that other size/date/time stuff to confuse the issue. There is, but first, let's clear the screen.

Clearing the Screen

When you or MS-DOS add something to a screen that's already filled, the contents of the screen scroll up a line at a time to make room at the bottom for the new text. The lines at the top disappear.

Look down the screen. See Strike a key when ready...? That was at the bottom of the screen a minute ago. The remainder of the directory ("page 2") did not have enough lines to fill the entire screen, so it just made room for itself at the bottom. In a minute, you'll be calling up another kind of directory, and that will push the existing screen up from the bottom. To make things less cluttered and to clear the screen of old business before introducing something new, type:

cls ENTER

...at the A> prompt. The old directory goes away, and the slate is clean.

To enable the **cls** command on the Tandy 1200, follow these steps:

1. Check the directory of the MS-DOS disk to see if the CONFIG.SYS file is listed. If it is NOT there, type:

   copy con config.sys ENTER
   device = ansi.sys ENTER

   If CONFIG.SYS is listed in the MS-DOS directory, type:

   copy config.sys + con ENTER
   device = ansi.sys ENTER

2. Press [Ctrl] [Z], then [ENTER].

3. Reset the computer by pressing [Ctrl] [Alt] [Del] and the 1200 is ready to use **cls**.

A Names-Only Directory

You added a short extension to the basic **dir** command to make it display one page at a time. There is another extension that makes it display a five-column-wide, all-across-the screen listing of file names only. Type:

dir/w [ENTER]

In this format, the screen can hold the entire directory of the MS-DOS disk because by leaving out some information, it can squeeze five names onto each line. The file type, COM, SYS, EXE, etc., is still included in this format because, as you'll learn a little later, these extensions are actually part of the name.

SUMMARY

* A disk is like a bookshelf; a file is like a book.
* Type **dir** to see a *directory*, or table of contents, of a disk.
* Type **dir/p** to see the directory one "page" at a time.
* Type **dir/w** ("wide directory") to see a names-only directory.
* Type **cls** to **c**lear the **s**creen.
* The 1200 requires a special one-time procedure (described in the text) to enable **cls**.

C H A P T E R 3

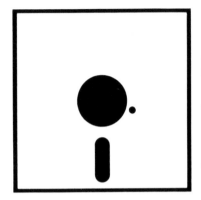

Printing
What's on
the Screen

There are several ways to print what's on the screen, and as you may have guessed if you studied the keyboard, they both use the [PRINT] key (the [Prt Sc] key on the 1200 and 3000s). To print exactly what's on the screen at this moment (which happens to be the wide version of the directory), press [SHIFT] [PRINT] (or [Shift] [Prt Sc]).

If your printer is hooked up and turned on, the wide-format directory should now be on paper. (If your printer is *not* ready, nothing will happen. The screen will freeze, and you won't be able to do anything until you get the printer on line. If, for some reason, you can't do that, wait a few seconds for the computer to return control to the keyboard, or press Reset (or [Ctrl] [Alt] [Del] on the 1200 and 3000s) to cancel the print order. If you reset the computer, use **dir/w** to display the directory again.)

Pressing the [PRINT] key without [SHIFT] produces a slightly different result. Used by itself, the [PRINT] key works as a "toggle" switch. That means pressing the key once turns the *print* function on, and pressing it again turns it off. (To toggle the print function on the 1200 and 3000s, press [Ctrl] [Prt Sc].)

Clear the screen again with **cls** [ENTER], and press [PRINT] ([Ctrl] [Prt Sc] on the 1200 and 3000s) once. Nothing seems to have happened, but now request a regular, long-form directory by typing **dir** [ENTER]. Watch as each line that is fed to the screen is also fed to the printer.

Type **cls** ENTER again. The screen clears, and if you look at the bottom of the printout, you'll see:

A>cls

...the system prompt and the new command you just typed. As long as the print function is toggled on, everything added to the screen will also be added to the printout. Printing takes place at each "carriage return." Try printing the one-page-at-a-time directory with **dir/p**. As soon as the first page is printed, press PRINT or Ctrl Prt Sc to shut off the printer, then any regular key to finish displaying the directory. Up it comes to the screen, but not to the printer.

Canceling a Command

Any command that can be typed onto the screen can be canceled in mid-execution with CTRL C. Find the CTRL and C keys on the keyboard. To do this correctly, you'll need to hold down the CTRL key while you tap the C, then let up on both. For a demonstration, type **dir**, but don't press ENTER yet. Get the fingers of your left hand poised over CTRL and C, then press ENTER with a finger of your right hand. When four or five lines of the directory have appeared on the screen, press CTRL C to stop it in its tracks.

Clear the screen and try it again, but this time add the printer. Toggle it on with the PRINT key. After a few lines are printed, press CTRL C to cancel the **dir** command. The directory will no longer be sent to either the screen *or* the printer.

CTRL C will not work with SHIFT PRINT or Shift Prt Sc. Try it. Press SHIFT PRINT, and when printing starts, press CTRL C to try to stop it. It won't. Just remember that CTRL C only cancels commands you type onto the screen.

Freezing a Command

Commands can also be temporarily suspended or "frozen." Type **dir** again to display another directory. This time press CTRL S. (If the keyboard has a HOLD key, you can use that.)

Like [CTRL] [C], [CTRL] [S] stopped the information displayed on the screen. But, unlike [CTRL] [C], the action can be continued; simply press [CTRL] [S] (or [HOLD]) a second time.

Using [CTRL] [S] is handy when displaying long directories or viewing text files (which we'll learn about later). To remember which control-key sequence is which, think of [CTRL] [C] as canceling and [CTRL] [S] as suspending a command.

SUMMARY

* Press [SHIFT] [PRINT] to print what's on the screen. On the 1200 and 3000s, press [Shift] [Prt Sc].
* Press [PRINT] to turn printer on, press again to turn it off. On the 1200 and 3000s, press [Ctrl] [Prt Sc]. With the printer turned on, everything that appears on the screen is printed as it appears.
* Press [CTRL] [C] to cancel a command that is visible on the screen.
* Press [CTRL] [S] (or [HOLD]) to suspend a command displayed on the screen. Press a second time to continue.

CHAPTER 4

Shutting Down the System

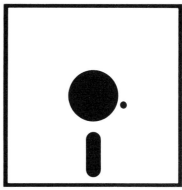

In the introduction we attempted to produce analogies to describe MS-DOS. Here's another one: think of MS-DOS as the computer's mother. It wakes the computer up, sends it off to school or work or play, keeps it organized, picks up after it, and at the end of the day, when the work is all done and everything has been put away, the computer returns to Mom and then shuts down for the night. Bet you never thought of it quite like that, but in its own corny way, it's true. MS-DOS should be the one that locks up for the night. When you finish working in some application or another, you shouldn't just hit the Big Switch. You should properly exit the program, get back home to MS-DOS and the A⟩ prompt, remove any floppy disks from their drives and *then* hit the Big Switch.

These comments about the floppies are pretty important. Since floppy and hard disks are magnetic surfaces on which information is stored by electrical impulses, they are sensitive to BIG electrical impulses. When an electronic device, like a computer, is turned off, it sometimes experiences an internal surge--a jolt of electricity in its circuits. That's perfectly normal and doesn't hurt the computer a bit, but if one of these surge currents should find its way to the sensitive surface of a disk or the recording head while the disk is spinning next to it, damage and/or lost data could result.

Remember this rule: take care of the diskettes before you touch the power switch. Are there any red lights lit up on the floppy drives? If so, wait until they go out before removing the disks. Is the "Active" light flashing on the hard drive? If so, wait until that goes out before shutting down the hard drive. If the hard drive is built-in, or plugged into the main plug strip along with the computer, it's okay to turn both off at the same time. Be sure disk drives' lights are off *before* turning anything off.

SUMMARY

* Remove diskettes from drives before turning power off.
* Turn off the hard drive before or at the same time as the computer.

CHAPTER 5

Review of Part One

The intent of Part One was to introduce you to the startup and shutdown procedures for MS-DOS. You've turned the computer on, set the date and time, checked the directory to see what's on the system disk, printed it out, cleared the screen and then shut everything down. You'll do most of these things every time you use the computer, so if anything is not clear, it would be wise to take another run through Part One before you go on.

MS-DOS is at your command. As long as it's not busy doing something else and the system prompt is on the screen with a flashing cursor, you can issue commands. You've learned some commands already, and you'll be learning many more as you proceed through this volume and the next. Some commands are carried out by the MS-DOS "system" itself. These tend to be the shorter, simpler ones; **date**, **cls** and **dir** are examples. Beginning with the next chapter, we'll look at commands that are complicated enough to require a whole file full of instructions. They won't be complicated to you, however; you'll just have to type in the name of the command. What MS-DOS has to go through to execute that command is its problem!

As mentioned in the Introduction, commands that MS-DOS can handle immediately, without loading one of the files on the disk, are called *internal* commands. Commands which require MS-DOS to load a file from the directory of MS-DOS programs we've been working with are called *external* commands. Right now it doesn't really matter much to you whether a particular command is internal or external, as long as it gets the job done. Later, it will.

17

Command Review

date displays current MS-DOS date and offers the opportunity to change it. Change can be bypassed with ENTER .

time displays current MS-DOS time and offers the opportunity to change it. Change can be bypassed with ENTER .

dir displays "table of contents" of a disk. Continues scrolling until bottom of directory appears on screen.

dir/p stops display of directory when screen is full. When finished reading first "page" of directory, press the space bar to see next page.

dir/w displays "wide" version of directory. Includes only names of files and their extensions in five columns across screen.

cls clears screen, leaving only system prompt. **cls** must be enabled on the Tandy 1200 before it can be used.

Keyboard Commands

CTRL C cancels execution of a typed command.

CTRL S (or HOLD) suspends a typed command. Pressing CTRL S (or HOLD) again continues it.

PRINT (Ctrl Prt Sc on the 1200 and 3000s) toggles on/off. Sends everything *going to* the screen also to the printer.

SHIFT PRINT (Shift Prt Sc on the 1200 and 3000s) sends everything *currently on* the screen to the printer. Commonly called a *screen dump*.

Notes

Startup   Turn on the computer, then insert the MS-DOS disk in Drive A.

Turn on hard drive before, or with same switch as, the computer.

Shutdown Remove disks and shut down hard drive before turning off the computer. The hard drive can be shut off with same switch as the computer.

PART 2

Using MS-DOS to prepare your diskettes

CHAPTER 6

Disk Drives

The Great Compatibility Question

Because this book covers many Tandy computers, let's take a moment to sort out which is which. Generally speaking, the 1000 Series and the 1200 are "compatible" with the IBM PC and XT. The 3000 Series is compatible with the IBM PC AT. This means that virtually all software that runs on IBMs will run on Tandy machines.

The Tandy 2000 is different from the rest because it's a much more powerful machine. Its floppy disks can store twice as much data, and it "computes" twice as fast as the 1000s and 1200.

Disk Capacities

In Chapter 2 we described a byte as the amount of memory required to store one character--a letter, number, space or punctuation mark. The amount of memory that came with your computer, 256K, 512K and so on, refers to the number of characters that can be loaded into the computer *at any one time*.

Suppose you have a 256K machine and you want to run a spreadsheet program which requires 56K of memory. The spreadsheet program includes all the instructions to the computer, the calculating space, and the screen formats, all of which is equivalent to 56 thousand characters. It all needs to be in the computer at the same time. That leaves room for up to 200 thousand numbers and letters for you to store as data in the spreadsheet. If any one of your spreadsheet projects--the profit/loss statement, the checking account ledger or whatever--gets bigger than 200 thousand characters, you'll need more memory.

This *volatile*, or *Random Access Memory* (RAM), is not the same as *disk* memory. When you are finished working with the profit/loss statement, for example, you can "save" it onto a disk, recording it for future use. Then it can be *cleared out of the computer*, freeing up 200K for the next spreadsheet. If the spreadsheet program itself is also cleared from memory, all 256K will be available for another application program.

While the computer can only work on 256K at any one time, the total amount of data you can have at hand and ready to access is limited only by the storage capacity of disks, multiplied by the number of disks you have. Using floppy disks gives us potentially infinite storage.

Each Tandy 1000, 1200, and 3000 HL floppy diskette is capable of storing approximately 360K. Because the 2000 is capable of packing the data more tightly onto the disk, a floppy in that machine can hold up to 720K. The 3-1/2" disks also hold 720K. The Tandy 3000 offers two options. Its floppy drive can use either a 360K sized disk or a 1,200K (called a 1.2 Megabyte) disk. This special 1.2M diskette is unique to the 3000 and cannot be read by a 1000, 1200, 2000, or 3000 HL. The 1.2M drive can, however, read 360K diskettes from the other Tandy MS-DOS computers.

All Tandy MS-DOS computers use "double-sided" diskettes. Data is stored on both sides; however, it's done automatically. You don't have to turn the diskette over or do anything else.

If you have a hard drive, it is not removable. Depending on the model, its total capacity will range from 10 to 70 million characters. How much is that? Counting every space and punctuation mark, a typical typewriten page contains about 3K (3000) characters. Ten million divided by 3K = 3333 pages. If that isn't enough, you'll need to add a second hard drive.

SUMMARY

* All Tandy MS-DOS computers, except the 2000, are "IBM compatible."
* Tandy 2000 has twice the disk capacity and works faster than the 1000s and 1200.
* The Tandy 3000 comes with a high capacity disk drive which uses 1.2 Megabyte floppy disks. It can also read 360K "standard" disks.
* Bytes of RAM are approximately the same as the amount of data that can be held in the computer at one time.
* When work on a file is finished, the file can be stored on a disk, then erased from RAM.
* Total disk storage capacity is limited only by the number of available disks.

CHAPTER 7

Formatting a Floppy Disk

The Format Command

Before any disk, floppy or hard, can be used to store data, it must be prepared by the computer. This preparation is called *formatting*. Floppy diskettes are formatted with the MS-DOS command: **format**. Formatting the hard drive is a little different and is covered in the next chapter.

If you're using the new 3-1/2" disks, refer to Chapter 10 for formatting information.

Start up the computer again, as you learned earlier. Insert the MS-DOS disk in Drive A and a blank disk, right out of the box, in Drive B. Be sure the labels on both disks are up and out.

When the A⟩ system prompt appears, type the command:

format b: ENTER

The **b:** at the end of the command tells MS-DOS that the diskette you want to format is in Drive B.

One-Drive Systems
On single-drive systems, just type **format** *unless you are using version 3.2.* In that case, you must type **format a:**. The computer will prompt you to:

```
Insert new diskette for drive A:
and strike any key when ready
```

(The message may vary slightly with the machine.)

Remove the MS-DOS disk, and insert a blank disk.

The **format** command is one of those "external" commands we mentioned that require MS-DOS to go to the DOS disk and find one of its files. If you glance at your printout of the directory, you'll see the FORMAT.COM program listed. An instruction appears on the screen:

```
Insert new diskette for drive B:
and strike any key when ready
```

3.2 Series users see the message:

```
And strike ENTER when ready
```

You've already inserted a new diskette in Drive B, so press any key.

By the way, "strike any key," which appears now and then in MS-DOS, is not strictly correct. Certain keys, like the [SHIFT] key and a couple of others, won't work for this. In practice, most people press [ENTER].

On the 1000, 1000 EX, and 2000 you are treated to a little graphic display to prove that FORMAT.COM is actually working. What it's doing is creating magnetic "tracks" on the disk, somewhat similar to phonograph-record tracks, and every time it creates another track, it checks it off on the screen. When the job is done, a message like this appears:

```
Format complete

    362496 bytes total disk space
    362496 bytes available on disk

Format another (Y/N)?
```

The 362496 is the "360K" we mentioned as the capacity of Tandy 1000 and 1200 diskettes. Tandy 2000 users will see 731136 bytes; 3000 users will see 1213952 bytes.

Press ⃞N for "no," and we'll format another diskette a slightly different way. Insert another new disk, and at the A⟩ prompt, type:

format/v b: ⃞ENTER (Single floppy users can just type **format/v**.)

3.2 Series users with *either* one or two floppy drives, type **format b:/v**. Single drive users will be prompted to swap disks.

Everything proceeds as above, but when the formatting is done, this message appears:

Volume label (11 characters, ENTER for none)?

Remember when we looked at the directory in Chapter 1 and encountered the message Volume in drive A has no label? That meant that the diskette had no name. Now, during formatting of the new diskette we have the opportunity to give this one a name. Type:

SAMPLE_DISK ⃞ENTER

This new disk is now named SAMPLE_DISK. The formatting process is complete, and Format another (Y/N)? appears on the screen. Press ⃞N and check the directory to see the disk name. Type:

dir b: ⃞ENTER

Single drive users will be prompted to swap disks again.

Don't worry about that File not found message. It didn't list any files because there aren't any yet.

Take the formatted disk out and prepare a label for it. It might be helpful to make a mark on the label to indicate that this disk is already formatted, so you won't get confused. Do this before affixing the label to the diskette. An alternative is to set up a specially marked box for blank diskettes that have been formatted.

Bad Tracks

Once in a while you'll get a bum diskette. For one reason or another, it will have a bad spot or two which just won't format. This doesn't happen nearly as much as it used to because of the generally improved quality of today's diskettes, but should MS-DOS encounter a stubborn place, it will skip over it and format the rest of the disk. The disk won't hold quite as much data, but it's still usable.

During formatting, the screen display will look something like this if an area that can't be formatted is encountered on the disk:

```
Formatting tracks
++++++++++++++++++++++++++++++++++?+++++++++

    362496 bytes total disk space
      5120 bytes in bad sectors
    357376 bytes available on disk
```

Tandy 1200 and 3000 Series users will simply see the number of bytes of total disk space, in bad sectors and available on disk.

In many cases, formatting a diskette with a bad spot will "take" on the second or third try; however if you're not in desperate need of the diskette, it's better to put it aside and take it back to your computer center for a replacement.

SUMMARY

* Preparing a disk to store data is called *formatting*.
* To format a disk in Drive B, type **format b:**.
* Typing **format/v** provides an opportunity to give the diskette a name.
* If MS-DOS encounters a bad spot on a diskette, it will format "around" it, but it's a good idea to replace that disk if possible.

CHAPTER 8

Formatting the Hard Drive

If you don't have a hard drive, skip ahead to Chapter 9.

A hard drive changes your life somewhat, but it doesn't entirely replace the floppy disk drive. You'll still need the floppy drive to introduce new software, to make backups of the hard drive (vitally important, and covered in Chapter 12), and to make "portable" copies of your files to carry to other computers. All the information in this book relating to floppies is important to you.

We mention this because, once you get the hard drive formatted, MS-DOS will be put on it along with your software programs and probably all of your files. It's easy to forget the need for floppies once you get rolling with a hard drive.

One Big Note for Hard Drive Users

The hard drive is Drive C. (The floppies, if you have two, are A and B, and should you add a second hard drive, it would be D.) Once MS-DOS is put on the hard drive, you make Drive C the *active*, or default, drive. This means that from this point forward, *your default system prompt will be* C⟩. Throughout the rest of the book, when we refer to the A⟩ prompt, you'll see the hard drive prompt, C⟩.

If this complicates things for you at all (you'll quickly get used to it), you'll be compensated by the fact that you don't normally have to bother with drive

30

designators at all. In other words, while floppy users are busy attaching **b:** to their file names and **a:** to the MS-DOS files, you'll be able to relax in the knowledge that everything you have is on the same drive. You won't have to worry about whether a command is *internal* or *external* because MS-DOS and all of its programs are present at all times.

FORMATTING THE TANDY 1000 HARD DRIVE (DOS 2.11)

If your hard drive is not built in, be sure that it's hooked up according to the instructions that came with it. Before turning on an external hard drive or a computer with a built-in hard drive, turn it upside down and locate the *Media Error Map* on the bottom. (DON'T ever turn the hard drive upside down while it's on.) Copy any numbers you find on the map to a piece of scratch paper and save it for later.

If they are not connected to a common switch, first turn on the hard drive, then the computer. Tandy recommends that you wait about 30 minutes for the hard drive to warm up before beginning the formatting procedure. This doesn't apply to normal use of the drive, just formatting.

Put the MS-DOS disk in Drive A and reset the computer. Enter the date and time as usual, and at the A⟩ prompt, remove the MS-DOS disk and insert the **Hard Disk Utilities** diskette that came with your hard drive. Type the first command:

hsect [ENTER]

The message will appear to:

Press any key to begin formatting drive C

Press the space bar and the first phase begins. MS-DOS will inform you that it is Formatting ..... and in a few minutes (two or three minutes for a 10-meg drive, around six minutes for a 15 meg), it will say Format completed! Don't get too excited, however, you're not finished yet.

Initializing the Hard Drive

Phase two of the procedure requires another command. When the Format completed! message appears and the A> prompt returns, type:

fdisk [ENTER]

The initialization Main Menu appears:

```
FDISK Options

Current Hard Disk Drive: 1

Choose one of the following:

        1.        Create DOS Partition
        2.        Change Active Partition
        3.        Delete DOS Partition
        4.        Display Partition Data
        5.        Select Next Hard Disk Drive
        6.        Select Previous Hard Disk Drive

Enter Selection -->

Press ESC to exit to MSDOS
```

Press [1] to Create DOS Partition. The next message is:

```
Create Dos Partition

Current Hard Disk Drive: 1

Do you wish to use the entire hard
disk for DOS (Y/N) --> Y
```

It's asking if you want to break the hard disk up into sections for special applications or use the entire thing for MS-DOS and MS-DOS files. You only want one partition for now, so press [Y].

The Main Menu appears again; this time press ④:

```
4.          Display Partition Data

Current Hard Disk Drive: 1

Partition     Status     Type     Start     End     Size
    1            N        DOS        0       304     305

Total hard drive space is 305 cylinders

Press any key to continue --------------->
```

This report tells you, briefly, that Partition number 1 is a "non-active" (we'll come back to that) partition, that it is configured for MS-DOS, and that it starts at cylinder 0 and extends to cylinder 304. Partition 1 uses 305 out of a total disk space of 305 cylinders. In other words, it takes up the whole disk.

The Status is the only thing we want to change. Non-active means that this is not the drive that the computer will automatically go to for instructions at boot-up time. You can change the default drive any time you want to by just typing its letter and a colon, but when you reset or turn the power on, MS-DOS always returns to Drive A and the A> prompt.

By changing the status of the hard drive to Active, guess what you're doing? You're fixing it so that the computer will boot up from the hard drive and automatically display the C> prompt. As we said at the beginning of this chapter, you'll be reading A> through the rest of this book, but on your screen, you'll be seeing C>. In just a moment, we're going to copy the MS-DOS diskette onto the hard drive, and after that, you won't need to use the MS-DOS floppy diskette at all.

Making the Hard Drive the Active Drive

So. On to changing the status. Press the space bar to get out of the status report and back into the Main Menu. Press ② to Change Active Partition:

```
2.          Change Active Partition
```

The status report reappears, along with the instruction:

Enter the number you want to make active

You only have one partition, and its number is 1, so press [1]. Once again the menu appears. Check the status one more time to see if the one-and-only partition has been changed to active. Do that by selecting item 4 on the Main Menu:

    4.   Display Partition Data

Back comes the status report, and sure enough, Status is now changed to A:

Partition	Status	Type	Start	End	Size
1	A	DOS	0	304	305

Press the space bar to get back to the Main Menu, then [ESC] to return to MS-DOS. A short beep and a message will tell you that:

System needs to reboot
Insert system disk in Drive A
Please reset the system

Put the MS-DOS diskette back in Drive A and press the Reset button.

Enter the date and time again, then remove the MS-DOS diskette and put the Hard Disk Utilities diskette back in the drive.

Finishing the Format Procedure

This may seem like a long process, but luckily, with a hard drive, you normally only have to do it once.

The next command prepares the disk to receive MS-DOS. Type:

hformat c: /s/v/b [ENTER]

The message on the screen is:

```
Insert DOS diskette in drive A:
and strike any key when ready
```

After replacing the utility disk with the DOS disk, press the space bar. The computer displays:

```
Enter next head, track pair or press <ENTER> to quit,
```

If your *Media Error Map* did not list any numbers, simply press [ENTER] to start the Format procedure. If, however, one or more Head and Cylinder error numbers were listed now is the time to report them to the computer (did you remember to jot them down earlier?). For example, if your listing showed:

```
     Head          Cylinder
      1               282
```

you should type in the numbers:

1,282 [ENTER]

Do this for each set of numbers that is listed on the *Media Error Map*. After the last pair of numbers is entered, press [ENTER]. (Most hard disks have one or more small bad spots on the disk. This is normal, and the manufacturer identifies the locations of these spots and writes them on the "Map" on the bottom of the disk drive. When you enter the locations, you are telling MS-DOS to format around them. Aside from a minute loss of storage capacity, the hard drive will operate as though the spots didn't even exist.)

Again, we are prompted to:

```
Press any key to begin formatting C:
```

Not the most appropriate message, since you already formatted Drive C once, but it's now going through a final phase of the formatting, so press the space bar to get it started. For this part of the format, a display is provided to keep you amused while you wait:

```
Formatting Cylinders...

+++++++++-------------------------------------------------
-----------------------------------------------------------
-------------- ...etc.
```

When finished, this message appears:

```
System transferred
Volume label (11 characters, ENTER for none)?
```

The format is complete, and the MS-DOS system is transferred to the hard drive. Now, how about a name for the hard disk? Type:

HARD_DISK [ENTER]

That seems appropriate. And at last:

```
Format complete
     10592256 bytes total disk space
        45056 bytes used by system
     10547200 bytes available on disk
```

Copying the MS-DOS Programs to the Hard Disk

All that remains is to copy the rest of the MS-DOS disk to the new Drive C. The **copy** command does the trick. Type:

copy a:*.* c: [ENTER]

This copies all files to the hard drive, and the job is done. When the copy is complete, remove the floppies and press the Reset button or shut off the computer and turn it back on again. The `C>` prompt should automatically appear, and you're in business.

FORMATTING THE TANDY 1200 HARD DRIVE

If your hard drive is not built in, be sure that it's hooked up according to the instructions that came with it. Before turning on an external hard drive or a computer with a built-in hard drive, turn it upside down and locate the *Media Error Map* on the bottom. (DON'T ever turn the hard drive upside down while it's on.) Copy any numbers you find on the map to a piece of scratch paper and save it for later.

If they are not connected to a common switch, first turn on the hard drive, then the computer. Tandy recommends that you wait about 30 minutes for the hard drive to warm up before beginning the formatting procedure. This doesn't apply to normal use of the drive, just formatting.

Put the MS-DOS disk in Drive A and reset the computer. Enter the date and time as usual, and at the A⟩ prompt, type the first command:

llfdfmt [ENTER]

MS-DOS will warn us that:

```
ALL DATA on the fixed disk will be DESTROYED
Do you want to continue (y or n) ?
```

The format procedure erases all data that may have been previously stored on the hard drive. At this point, we haven't used the hard drive yet so there is no data to lose. Answer the question by typing **y**.

The next question is:

```
Which fixed disk to format (C or D) ?
```

As discussed earlier, the hard drive is normally designated as Drive C so answer the question by typing **c**.

The message:

```
Press any key when ready (Ctrl-Break to abort)
```

will appear.

Press the space bar, and the first phase begins. MS-DOS will inform you that it is:

```
Formatting fixed disk  c: allow one hour for completion
```

In about 30 minutes the first phase of the procedure will be complete, and MS-DOS will report:

```
Format complete, no areas deleted
```

```
Are there any areas to manually delete ? (y or n)
```

If your *Media Error Map* did not list any numbers, answer by typing **n**. If, however, one or more Head and Cylinder error numbers were listed now is the time to report them to the computer (did you remember to jot them down earlier?). Type **y** and enter the numbers under the appropriate headings. For example:

```
Head            Cylinder        Degree       Enter 'd' if last entry
  1                126             339
```

Press [ENTER] after entering each number. If your hard drive has more than one Media Error listing, press [ENTER] twice to move to the next line. Do this for each set of numbers that is listed on the *Media Error Map*. After the last set of numbers is entered, type **d** (you must use lower case) and see the message:

```
Format complete, returning to DOS,
```

Don't get too excited, however, you're not finished yet.

Partitioning the Hard Drive

Phase two of the procedure requires another command. When the A> prompt returns, type:

part [ENTER]

The PARTition Menu appears:

```
PART Options
  Choose one of the following:

        1.          Display Partition Data
        2.          Change Active Partition
        3.          Delete DOS Partition
        4.          Create DOS Partition

  Enter choice:   [1]

  Enter ESC to exit to DOS
```

Ignore the default entry [1] provided by the computer and press 4 ENTER to Create DOS Partition. The next message is:

```
Create DOS Partition

Do you wish to use the entire
Winchester disk for DOS (Y/N)? [Y]
```

It's asking if you want to break the hard disk up into sections for special applications or use the entire thing for MS-DOS and MS-DOS files. You only want one partition for now, so press ENTER to accept the [Y] default answer.

The DOS Partition report appears:

```
Create DOS Partition


Partition Status  Type  Start End  Size
     1        A     DOS    0    304  305

Total Hard disk space is 305 cylinders


Enter ESC to return to Menu
```

This report tells you, briefly, that Partition number 1 is an "Active" partition, that it is configured for MS-DOS, and that it starts at cylinder 0 and extends to cylinder 304. Partition 1 uses 305 out of a total disk space of 305 cylinders. In other words, it takes up the whole disk.

Press [Esc] to return to the PARTition Menu, then press [Esc] again to see the message:

```
System must now be Rebooted
Insert a DOS diskette in Drive A:
and strike any key

( If you are using PREPARE, you must
  reload it after reboot to complete
  the hard drive installation. )
```

With the MS-DOS diskette still in Drive A, press the space bar to return to MS-DOS.

Enter the date and time again.

Finishing the Format Procedure

This may seem like a long process, but luckily, with a hard drive, you normally only have to do it once.

The next command prepares the disk to receive MS-DOS. Type:

format c: /s/f [ENTER]

The message on the screen is:

```
Press any key to begin formatting fixed disk C:
```

Not the most appropriate message, since you already formatted Drive C once, but it's now going through a final phase of the formatting, so press the space bar to get it started.

```
Formatting drive C: ....
```

This procedure takes about 2 minutes. And at last, this message:

```
Format Complete
System transferred

 10593280 bytes total disk space
    42162 bytes in system files
 10551118 bytes available on disk
```

Copying the MS-DOS Programs to the Hard Disk

All that remains is to copy the rest of the MS-DOS disk to the new Drive C. The **copy** command does the trick. Type:

copy a:*.* c: [ENTER]

This copies all files to the hard drive.

Switch the default drive to C by typing:

c: [ENTER]

The `C>` prompt should appear, and you're in business.

FORMATTING THE TANDY 2000 HARD DRIVE

If your hard drive is not built in, be sure that it's hooked up according to the instructions that came with it. Before turning on an external hard drive or a computer with a built-in hard drive, turn it upside down and locate the *Media Error Map* on the bottom. (DON'T ever turn the hard drive upside down while it's on.) Copy any numbers you find on the map to a piece of scratch paper and save it for later.

If they are not connected to a common switch, first turn on the hard drive, then the computer. Tandy recommends that you wait about 30 minutes for the hard drive to warm up before beginning the formatting procedure. This doesn't apply to normal use of the drive, just formatting.

Put the MS-DOS disk in Drive A and reset the computer. Enter the date and time as usual, and at the A> prompt, type the first command:

confighd `ENTER`

hformat /s/b appears briefly. Then the screen clears, and the copyright notice appears, along with the following message:

Enter next head, track pair or press <ENTER> to quit.

The Media Error Map

Enter the Head and Track numbers from the *Media Error Map* attached to the bottom of the computer or external drive. (DON'T turn the computer or drive upside down while it's running! Check the list you made earlier.) For example:

3,276 `ENTER`
2,170 `ENTER`

Press `ENTER` again when the last Head/Track number has been entered or press `ENTER` if the *Media Error Map* is blank.

Starting the Formatting

The computer then asks you to:

Press any key to begin formatting C:

Press the space bar and watch the display as each cylinder is formatted.

Formatting cylinders

. . . --

----------------- ...etc.

When finished, this message appears:

```
System transferred

Format complete

10616832  bytes total disk space
   73728  bytes used by system
10543104  bytes available on disk

A>copy a:*.* c:
```

followed by the name of each MS-DOS file as it is copied from Drive A to Drive C. MS-DOS tells you when all the files have been copied by displaying:

```
   33 Files(s) copied
```

The hard drive is now formatted, and MS-DOS (all 33 files of it) has been copied over to it. Your "active" drive is now Drive C--the hard drive. Whenever you turn on or reset the computer, control will automatically go to Drive C, and the C> prompt will appear. You can remove the MS-DOS floppy disk from Drive A and put it away.

FORMATTING THE 3.2 SERIES COMPUTER HARD DRIVE*

If your hard drive is not built in, be sure that it's hooked up according to the instructions that came with it. Before turning on an external hard drive or a computer with a built-in hard drive, locate the *Media Error Map*. It could be on the bottom, or if the drive's internal, inside the computer itself. (DON'T ever turn the hard drive upside down while it's on.) Copy any numbers you find on the map to a piece of scratch paper and save it for later.

If the computer and hard drive are not connected to a common switch, first turn on the hard drive, then the computer. Internal hard drives start when the computer is turned on.

---

* This procedure applies only to standard hard drives of 32 or fewer Meg. Check the MS-DOS manual that came with your computer to see which drives are standard and which formatting procedure are used for larger and/ or nonstandard hard drives.

NOTE: **3000 Series users, if you configured your system for a hard drive during the SETUP procedure, skip to "Initializing the Hard Drive."**

Put the MS-DOS disk in Drive A and boot the computer. Press ENTER at the date and time prompts. At the A> prompt, remove the MS-DOS disk and insert the **Supplemental Programs** diskette that came with the MS-DOS manual. Type the first command:

hsect ENTER

and when asked Which hard drive do you want to format (C/D)?, press C ENTER. At this point you don't have anything on the hard drive yet, so you can ignore the warning:

```
ALL data on drive C will be DESTROYED!!
Do you want to continue (Y/N)
?
```

Press Y ENTER.

```
Do you want to flag defective tracks (Y/N)
?
```

If your *Media Error Map* did not list any numbers, simply press N ENTER. If, however, one or more Head and Cylinder error numbers were listed, now is the time to report them to the computer (did you remember to jot them down earlier?). Press Y ENTER and follow the instructions on the screen.

The next message instructs:

```
Enter interleave factor
Press <enter> to use default value 5.
Valid values are 2-8
?
```

Accept the default by pressing ENTER, and MS-DOS will inform you that it is Formatting...... In a few minutes, it will say Format completed! Don't get too excited, however, you're not finished yet.

Initializing the Hard Drive

To begin this part of the format process, type:

fdisk [ENTER]

The initialization Main Menu appears:

```
Choose one of the following:

    1.     Create DOS Partition
    2.     Change Active Partition
    3.     Delete DOS Partition
    4.     Display Partition Data
    5.     Select Next Hard Disk Drive
    6.     Select Previous Hard Disk Drive


Enter Selection -->

Press ESC to exit to MSDOS.
```

Press [1] [ENTER] to Create DOS Partition.

```
Do you wish to use the entire hard
disk for DOS (Y/N) --> Y
```

It's asking if you want to break the hard disk up into sections for special applications, for example XENIX, or use the entire thing for MS-DOS and MS-DOS files. You want one partition for now, so press [Y] [ENTER].

The computer displays:

```
System needs to reboot
Insert system disk in Drive A
Press any key to reset the system_
```

Replace the Supplemental Programs disk with the MS-DOS disk and press the space bar. Once the system is reset, press [ENTER] for the date and time prompts.

Finishing the Format Procedure

This may seem like a long process, but luckily, with a hard drive, you normally only have to do it once.

The next command prepares the disk to receive MS-DOS. Type:

format c: /s/v [ENTER]

The message on the screen is:

```
WARNING, ALL DATA ON NON-REMOVABLE DISK
DRIVE C: WILL BE LOST!
Proceed with Format (Y/N)?_
```

Press [Y], then [ENTER]. During this part of the format, numbers corresponding to the heads and cylinders are displayed as they are formatted.

When finished, this message appears:

```
Format complete
System transferred

Volume label (11 characters, ENTER for none)?
```

The format is complete, and the MS-DOS system is transferred to the hard drive. Now, how about a name for the hard disk? Type:

HARD_DISK [ENTER]

Copying the MS-DOS Programs to the Hard Disk

All that remains is to copy the rest of the MS-DOS disk to the new Drive C. The **copy** command does the trick. Type:

copy a:*.* c: [ENTER]

This copies all files to the hard drive.

Switch the default drive to C by typing:

c: [ENTER]

The C⟩ prompt should appear, and you're in business.

SUMMARY

* Your active drive will now be the hard drive, Drive C.

* When the book refers to the A⟩ prompt, you will generally see the C⟩ prompt.

FORMATTING THE TANDY 1000 HARD DRIVE (DOS 2.11)

1. Copy the numbers from the *Media Error Map* on the bottom of the computer or external drive. Do this with the power off.
2. At the A⟩ prompt, replace MS-DOS disk with Hard Disk Utilities diskette.
3. Type **hsect** [ENTER].
4. Press the space bar.
5. When the A⟩ prompt returns, type **fdisk** [ENTER].
6. Press [1] to create DOS partition.
7. Press [Y] to use entire hard disk for MS-DOS.
8. Press [2] to change the active partition.
9. Press [1] to make partition 1 active.
10. Press [4] to check status.
11. Press the space bar to return to the Main Menu.
12. Press [ESC] to return to MS-DOS.
13. Replace the Utilities disk in Drive A with the MS-DOS disk, and press the Reset button.
14. Enter date and time, then switch disks again.
15. Type **hformat c: /s/v/b** [ENTER].
16. Switch disks once more, and press the space bar.
17. Press [ENTER] if there were no media errors. If there were errors, enter the Head and Cylinder numbers copied from the map (step 1).
18. Press [ENTER] after each head/cylinder pair.
19. Press [ENTER] again after all errors are entered.
20. Press the space bar to complete formatting.
21. When prompted, type **HARD_DISK** [ENTER] to give name to the drive.
22. With the MS-DOS disk still in Drive A, type **copy a:*.* c:** [ENTER].
23. Remove floppies and press the Reset button to bring up the C⟩ prompt.

FORMATTING THE TANDY 1200 HARD DRIVE

1. Copy the numbers from the *Media Error Map* on the bottom of the computer or external drive. Do this with the power off.
2. At the A> prompt, type **llfdfmt** [ENTER].
3. Press [Y] to start formatting.
4. Press [C] to select Drive C.
5. Press the space bar to start phase one.
6. Press [N] if there were no media errors and go to step 10.
7. Press [Y] if there were errors. Enter the Head, Cylinder and Degree numbers copied from the map (step 1).
8. Press [ENTER] after each head/cylinder/degree entry.
9. Press [ENTER] twice after typing in the degree number if there is more than one media error to enter.
10. Type **d** after all errors are entered.
11. At the A> prompt, type **part** [ENTER].
12. Press [4] [ENTER] to create DOS partition.
13. Press [ENTER] to accept the [Y] default.
14. Press [Esc] twice and then the space bar to return to MS-DOS.
15. Enter the date and time.
16. Type **format c: /s/f** [ENTER] to complete the format procedure.
17. Press the space bar to start the last phase.
18. Type **copy a:*.* c:** [ENTER] to copy all files to the hard disk.
19. Type **c:** [ENTER] to bring up C> prompt.

FORMATTING THE TANDY 2000 HARD DRIVE

1. Copy the numbers from the *Media Error Map* on the bottom of the computer or external drive. Do this with the power off.
2. At the A> prompt, type **confighd** [ENTER].
3. Press [ENTER] if there were no media errors.
4. If there were errors, enter the Head and Track numbers copied from the map (step 1).
5. Press [ENTER] after each head/track pair.
6. Press [ENTER] again after all errors are entered.
7. Press the space bar to start formatting.
8. Remove the MS-DOS disk, and press the Reset button to bring up the C> prompt.

FORMATTING THE 3.2 SERIES COMPUTER HARD DRIVE
(Procedure for standard hard drives of 32 or fewer Meg)

1. Copy the numbers from the *Media Error Map*. Do this with the power off.
2. At the A⟩ prompt, type **hsect** [ENTER].
3. Press [C] [ENTER] to select Drive C as the one to format.
4. Press [Y] [ENTER] to start formatting.
5. Press [N] [ENTER] if there were no media errors and go to step 7.
6. Press [Y] [ENTER] if there were errors and follow the instructions on the screen.
7. Press [ENTER] to accept the default interleave value.
8. At the A⟩ prompt, replace the MS-DOS disk with the Supplemental Programs diskette.
9. Type **fdisk** [ENTER].
10. Press [1] [ENTER] to create DOS partition.
11. Press [Y] [ENTER] to use the entire hard disk for MS-DOS.
12. Replace the Supplemental Programs disk in Drive A with the MS-DOS disk, and press the space bar.
13. Press [ENTER] for the date and time.
14. Type **format c:** /s/v [ENTER].
15. Press [Y] [ENTER] to continue formatting.
16. When prompted, type **HARD_DISK** [ENTER] to give a name to the drive.
17. Type **copy a:*.* c:** [ENTER] to copy MS-DOS files to Drive C.
18. Type **c:** [ENTER] to make Drive C the default drive.

CHAPTER 9

Disk Protection

Diskettes are somewhat fragile for several reasons: 1) because information is stored on them by magnetic impulses and 2) because, unlike your favorite stereo tapes, every little "impulse" counts. You'd probably never notice the loss of one or two notes of music from a tape, but if one or two of the wrong bytes on a computer disk get erased or changed, the entire program could be rendered useless. The damaged characters may be in the instructions that make the program run, and a computer won't ad-lib; if a detailed instruction is missing one or two characters, it usually just won't work.

Most diskettes are protected from damage by things you type at the keyboard if a small adhesive strip called a *write-protect tab* covers the notch in the side of the disk. (See fig. 9-1.)

WRITE-
PROTECT
NOTCH

WRITE-PROTECT
"TAB" COVERS
NOTCH *and*
PREVENTS RE-
CORDING ONTO
DISK

Figure 9-1

The 3-1/2" diskettes use a special *write-protect locking mechanism*. Locate the tiny tile and hole on the disk as shown in figure 9-2.

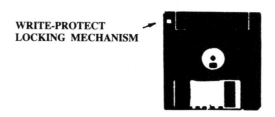

Figure 9-2

When the tile is positioned over the hole, the disk is *not* write protected--data *can* be written to the disk. Sliding the tile away from the hole turns write protection on--data *can't* be written to or erased from the disk.

Some external hard drives are protected with a red button on the front panel. (See fig. 9-3.) Press the button and it lights up, indicating that information can be *read* from the hard drive, but no new information can be *written to* it. Press the button again to turn protection off. Built-in hard drives do not usually have write protection.

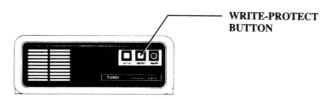

Figure 9-3

A write-protect tab or switch prevents any new information from being saved onto the disk. The MS-DOS disk should wear one at all times. Data diskettes, on the other hand, must not have tabs installed because you *want* to save data on them. While a write-protect tab can protect a disk from being recorded over, it doesn't protect it from other kinds of damage, so a copy, or "backup," should be made of all important disks. More on that, soon.

SUMMARY

* A write-protect tab prevents the computer from saving (recording) anything new on the diskette. Existing contents are protected from erasure and over-writing.
* To write protect 3-1/2" disks, slide the tile to expose the tiny hole on the disk. When the tile is *not* covering the hole, the disk is write-protected.
* Some external hard drives use a red button for protection. Internal hard drives are usually not write or erasure protected.
* A protected disk can be read from, but not written to.

CHAPTER 10

MS-DOS Floppy Format Fundamentals

Each different Tandy MS-DOS computer uses a distinct version of the same operating system (MS-DOS), and they all respond to very similar commands. However, when a computer with one floppy disk format tries to read files and data saved on a floppy disk from a computer using a different format, compatibility problems arise.

We've discovered three floppy disk formats so far:

    Tandy 1000 Series/1200/3000 HL = 360K bytes/diskette
    Tandy 2000 = 720K bytes/diskette
    Tandy 3000 = 1.2M or Megabytes (1,200K bytes)/diskette

The optional 3-1/2" disks are unique in their formats. These diskettes are covered in a separate section at the end of this chapter.

The 360K diskettes are the industry standard at this time. Almost all MS-DOS software is supplied on them, and they can be read by *all* Tandy MS-DOS computers.

The Tandy 2000's 720K format is unique, and 720K disks formatted on the 2000 can only be read by a 2000. The Tandy 3000's disks are compatible with the high capacity 1.2M diskettes used by the IBM PC AT and other high performance computers. Because of the Tandy 3000 and 2000's "high density" disk formats, for best reliability, special "high density" diskettes must be used.

MS-DOS Computer	Diskette Format
Tandy 1000 Series	360K
Tandy 1200	360K
Tandy 3000 HL	360K
IBM PC, XT	360K
Tandy 2000	720K
Tandy 3000	1.2M
IBM PC AT	1.2M

Special Tandy 3000 Considerations

The Tandy 3000 can format both 1.2M and 360K diskettes in its high capacity 1.2M disk drive. The **format** command, when used by itself, formats the special high density diskettes in the 1.2M mode. **format /4** formats standard diskettes in the 360K mode, as a standard 360K drive would. This capability leads to some interesting possibilities.

Suppose you use a Tandy 1000 at home and a Tandy 3000 at the office. You wish to review and edit a contract at home, but it is stored on the hard disk in the office 3000, which is equipped with a 1.2M floppy drive. How can you take the contract home for editing?

Easy. Insert an ordinary 360K floppy in the 1.2M drive and type **format /4**. After formatting, copy the contract from the hard disk to the 360K floppy. Take it home, insert it into your Tandy 1000, edit the contract as desired, and save the new version on the 360K diskette. The next day, take the diskette back to the office, and copy the edited contract back to the 3000's hard disk. (You will learn how to copy in later chapters.)

You should be aware that at this writing an industry-wide disk drive compatibility problem exists which (fortunately) doesn't normally affect Tandy computers. Specifically, most 360K diskettes formatted on a 1.2M drive are *not* readable by regular 360K drives. This problem negates the advantage of being able to use the 1.2M drive to format 360K diskettes and to write to them. This industry problem does *not* affect a 1.2M drive's ability to *read* 360K diskettes formatted on regular 360K drives, but writing to one may "glitch" it.

The most satisfactory overall solution is one which will also give your Tandy 3000 added versatility and flexibility. Add Drive B, a 360K second floppy drive (Radio Shack Cat. No. 25-4050). The 1.2M drive can then be reserved for storing large quantities of data, for transferring data between machines with 1.2M drives, and for making safety backups of the hard disk.

To demonstrate the "dual formatting" feature of the 1.2M drive, insert an ordinary double-sided, double-density diskette, and type:

format /4 [ENTER]

Since the magnetic characteristics of the 1.2M and 360K diskettes are different, it is important to carefully select the diskette which matches the format. Mixing up diskettes can generate substantial quantities of stomach acid.

Which Is Which?

This chart shows which diskettes can be read by which computers.

	Formatted by:					
	Tandy 1000 Series (360K)	Tandy 1200 (360K)	Tandy 2000 (720K)	Tandy* 2000 (360K)	Tandy 3000 Series (360K)	Tandy 3000 (1.2M)
Read by: Tandy 1000 Series	X	X		X	X	
Tandy 1200	X	X		X	X	
Tandy 2000	X	X	X	X	X	
Tandy 3000 HL	X	X		X	X	
Tandy 3000	X	X		X	X	X

* The Tandy 2000 can format 360K diskettes for use in other MS-DOS computers using a special program called PCMAKER.COM found on the 2000's system disk. PCMAKER follows the same rules as the **format** command.

The 3-1/2" Disk

The new 3-1/2" disk is now an option with many Tandy MS-DOS computers. This disk format is more compact than the standard 5-1/4" diskettes and holds more information. Also, because the diskette media is contained in a hard plastic shell, it's hard to accidentally fold, spindle or mutilate the disk. Taking work home from the office is as easy as dropping the disk into your pocket.

The 3-1/2" diskette holds 720K, or *twice* the information of a standard 5-1/4" floppy disk. The format of this disk is unique. And because of the smaller, compact 3-1/2" disk drives, 3-1/2" diskettes are only compatible with other MS-DOS 3-1/2" diskettes. A standard floppy drive cannot read from or write to a 3-1/2" disk--it's physically impossible.

These diskettes can be formatted using the same **format** command as used for any other MS-DOS disk. Internally, the computer hardware reports the size of the diskette to MS-DOS, which passes the information on to the FORMAT program. The 3-1/2" diskette is formatted automatically, without any special formatting options.

For example, if Drive B is the 3-1/2" drive, type:

format b:

The 3-1/2" disk will be formatted, and MS-DOS will report:

```
Format complete

   724992 bytes total disk space
   724992 bytes available on disk

Format another (Y/N)?
```

Type **N**. The diskette is now formatted and ready for use. Later, we'll learn how to copy files to and from this specially formatted diskette. Other than its unique size and greater storage capacity, simply consider this disk another member of the family.

Summary

* Tandy MS-DOS computers use three different floppy disk formats: 360K, 720K and 1.2M.

* All Tandy MS-DOS computers can read files and data from a standard 360K diskette.

* The 1.2M diskettes formatted in the Tandy 3000's 1.2M drive may only be read by a computer equipped with high capacity drives. 360K diskettes formatted by the 3000 are compatible with **all** Tandy's MS-DOS computers.

* To create a 360K formatted disk on the Tandy 3000, use **format /4**.

* The 2000's PCMAKER.COM program can be used in place of **format** to create 360K disks in the 2000's 720K drives.

* The optional 3-1/2" disk holds 720K of information. Though this diskette is incompatible with 5-1/4" disks, all Tandy MS-DOS computers with the 3-1/2" disk drive feature read the same 3-1/2" diskette format.

CHAPTER 11

Making Copies of Floppy Disks

Copying the MS-DOS Diskette

The first thing you'll want to do with one of your newly-formatted diskettes is make a duplicate copy of the MS-DOS disk. Once copied, this duplicate should become your working copy of MS-DOS. The original should be stored away in a safe place and only used again to make a new working copy should something happen to the first.

With the write-protected MS-DOS disk in Drive A, a formatted diskette in Drive B (no tab on this one) and the A> system prompt on the screen, type:

diskcopy a: b: [ENTER] (The spaces after the command and after the **a:** are
mandatory.)

MS-DOS advises you to:

```
Insert source diskette in drive A:
Insert target diskette in drive B:
Strike any key when ready
```

One-Drive Systems
Since you don't have two drives, there is no need to specify any; simply type **diskcopy** [ENTER], and this or a similar prompt appears:

```
Insert source diskette in drive A:
Strike ENTER when ready
```

3-1/2" Disk Drive

If Drive B is a 3-1/2" disk drive, **diskcopy** will not work. Use the **copy** command to make copies between 5-1/4" disks and 3-1/2" disks. See "Copying an Entire Disk Using the Wildcard" in Chapter 19 for specific instructions.

The disks are already inserted, so press [ENTER]. The computer reports that it is:

```
Copying...
```

and in a moment...

```
Copy complete
```

```
Copy another (Y/N)?
```

Press [N] to return to the A> prompt. MS-DOS copied everything from the disk in Drive A to the disk in Drive B, producing two identical disks. Put the original away, and use the copy in your day-to-day operations. The new working copy should also be treated to a write-protect tab.

One-Drive Systems

Making duplicate disks with a single disk drive necessitates some disk swapping. You may have noticed that shortly after you inserted the formatted source disk in your one-and-only floppy drive, a new prompt appeared:

```
Insert target diskette in drive A:
Strike any key when ready
```

MS-DOS will ask you to insert first one disk, then the other for a while as it "memorizes" a block of data from the source disk, then records it onto the target disk. Since a disk usually holds more than the computer itself can hold in RAM, a single-drive diskcopy must be done in stages.

Because the Tandy 3000's disks can have two formats, 1.2M "high density" or 360K "standard," some interesting problems can crop up when using **diskcopy**. For example, if an attempt is made to diskcopy a 360K disk to a formatted 1.2M disk, the following message appears:

```
Target media is bad, or not compatible with source format
```

Because of this, it's a good idea to always have 360K formatted diskettes available. If you have not already done so, use **format/4** to create a 360K disk on the Tandy 3000. Type:

format a:/4

Label the newly formatted disk as 360K, and keep it separate from 1.2M diskettes you have formatted. Use **diskcopy** and the 360K disk to make a copy of the MS-DOS disk. Save the 1.2M diskettes for storing data and miscellaneous files.

Copying a Data Disk

A data disk (one that contains information created by you) is copied with the same command (**diskcopy**) using the same procedure as for copying the MS-DOS disk. The only difference is that when prompted to `Insert source disk`, you must remove the MS-DOS disk and insert the disk you want copied. The target disk is still a blank, formatted disk. We haven't put anything on a data disk yet, so we'll hold off copying one until we have something interesting to copy.

Checking a Diskette's Name, or "Volume Label"

The command to check the name of a disk is **vol**. The MS-DOS disk has no name, and if you type **vol a:** you'll see the message you've seen before:

```
Volume in drive A has no label
```

Put the formatted disk you named "SAMPLE_DISK" in Drive B (or, if you only have one drive, replace the MS-DOS disk in Drive A) and type:

vol b: [ENTER] (just **vol** [ENTER] if you have one drive...)

Now the name SAMPLE_DISK appears. If you have multiple drives or a hard disk, this is a handy way to check which disk is where. Once a disk is named, it can't be renamed by MS-DOS unless it is reformatted. Since reformatting will erase the contents of the disk, it really becomes a new disk, with a new name.

Label (version 3.1 and higher)

MS-DOS versions 3.1 and higher include a special command which allows a diskette's name to be changed *after* a disk is formatted. The **label** command can add, change, or delete a diskette's volume label.

Let's see how it works. With your MS-DOS disk in Drive A, type:

label [ENTER]

If your system disk already had a name, it would be displayed. Since it doesn't, the screen shows:

```
Volume in drive A has no label

Volume label (11 characters, ENTER for none)?
```

Type:

SYSTEM_DISK [ENTER]

The new label will be "affixed" to the disk and appear every time you display its directory. Go ahead and check. Type **dir** [ENTER].

To change a label, simply type **label**, and when prompted, type in the *new* label. Try it. Type:

label [ENTER]

When the following appears:

```
Volume in drive A is SYSTEM_DISK

Volume label (11 characters, ENTER for none)?
```

Type:

MS_DOS_DISK [ENTER]

Now let's remove the label. Type **label** [ENTER] and instead of typing in a new label, press [ENTER]. When MS-DOS asks for confirmation:

`Delete current volume label (Y/N)?`

press [Y] [ENTER], and your disk will no longer have a name.

The **label** command can be followed by a disk drive designation so a volume label can be changed on a disk in any drive. For example, typing:

label b: [ENTER]

allows you to make changes to the diskette in Drive B. (If you decide to try this using the disk named SAMPLE_DISK, be sure to rename it SAMPLE_DISK when you're done. We'll be referring to that volume label in later chapters.)

For DOS 2.11 users there are special "utility" programs which can assign or delete volume labels. Ask your dealer.

SUMMARY

* The original MS-DOS disk should be kept in a safe place. Use copies for day-to-day operation.
* Type **diskcopy a: b:** to copy the disk in Drive A onto a formatted blank disk in Drive B. (Single floppy drive users type only **diskcopy**.)
* Use **copy** to make copies between 3-1/2" and 5-1/4" disks.
* On the Tandy 3000, only diskettes of the same format (360K or 1.2M) can be diskcopied to each other.
* Copy data diskettes the same way as the MS-DOS disk, except, when prompted to insert the *source* disk, remove the MS-DOS disk and insert the disk you want to copy.
* Type **vol a:** to check the name of the disk in Drive A.
* Type **label a:** to add, change, or delete the volume label of a disk in Drive A (version 3.1 and higher).

CHAPTER 12

Backing Up the Hard Drive

If you don't have a hard drive, go on to Chapter 13.

The primary purpose of making a backup of the hard drive is for security-- so that a copy of the information will exist in the event of some sort of catastrophic hard disk failure. Making backups is one of the most important things you will do with your computer. In the normal course of operation you'll be provided with all kinds of opportunities to make mistakes (like tripping over the power cord) and without backups, an awful lot of work can disappear.

There are two operations covered in this chapter: 1. moving information from the hard disk to a floppy, which requires the **backup** command, and 2. moving information from a floppy to the hard disk. This second procedure requires the **restore** command.

Keep in mind that **backup** and **restore** are used primarily to save, or "archive," valuable files and data on the hard drive. Later on, in Chapter 18, we'll discuss the standard way of *copying* files to and from different disk drives.

MAKING BACKUPS OF THE TANDY 1000 HARD DISK (DOS 2.11)

The **backup** and **restore** commands need to be copied onto the hard drive from the Hard Disk Utilities diskette. Place the Hard Disk Utilities diskette in Drive A and type:

copy a:backup.exe c: ENTER

Then type:

copy a:restore.exe c: [ENTER]

Backing Up Files* *from* the Hard Disk

You'll need two formatted, blank disks. Place one in Drive A and at the C⟩ prompt, type:

backup c: a: [ENTER]

The computer displays the warning:

```
Warning:  All Files will be Deleted on Destination Diskette
Please Insert Backup Diskette into Drive A:
Strike Any Key to CONTINUE
```

MS-DOS is providing the opportunity to change your mind before it starts the backup procedure. It is warning that any files that may already be on Drive A's disk will be erased during the backup.

You already have a formatted disk in Drive A so press [ENTER] to start the backup.

The screen lists each file's name as it is being backed up from Drive C to Drive A. When the first disk is full, the computer instructs:

```
Insert Next Backup Diskette
Strike any Key to CONTINUE
```

and displays the same warning message. Replace the full disk with a second formatted, blank disk and press [ENTER]. After all files have been backed up to the floppy disk, the computer reports:

---

* A file is the working unit of information storage. They were compared to "books on a bookshelf" in Chapter 2. All the chapters in Part Three of this book are concerned with files, so you'll become well acquainted with them.

```
Total number of File(s) Backed Up                    39
```

Backing Up One File

Should you want the floppy backup disk to contain only one of the files currently on the hard drive, specify the file's name after the **backup** command. For example, with the *first* backup disk in Drive A, type:

backup c:print.com a: `ENTER`

The warning message is displayed again, indicating that even a single file will cause all existing files on the floppy to be erased. The screen displays the file name PRINT.COM and indicates:

```
Total number of File(s) Backed Up                     1
```

Check the directory of Drive A. Remember that "whole bunch of files" that used to be on Drive A? All that remains on it is the file we asked for (PRINT.COM) and the file BACKUPID.@@@. (The computer generated this last file as part of the backup procedure.)

Adding a File to the Backup Disk

It is possible to add individual files to the backup floppy without erasing everything on it. This time let's backup the file SORT.EXE without losing the PRINT.COM file. Type:

backup c:sort.exe a:/a `ENTER`

Check the Drive A directory again. By adding the **/a** at the end of the **backup** command MS-DOS *copied* SORT.EXE from the default Drive (C) to Drive A and added it to what was already on that disk.

Backing Up by Date

Whenever a file is created or modified, a date shows up on the directory. (That's what all those dates in the directory are.) A handy backup feature is the ability to back up only those files dated on or after a certain date. Suppose, for example, you wanted to backup all files that were created or modified on Drive C on or after May 1, 1986. Type:

backup c: a:/d:Ø5/Ø1/86 [ENTER]

...and press [ENTER] after the warning message. When the backup is complete check the directory of Drive A. Notice that the date for each file is later than 5-Ø1-86.

Another variation of the command is used to backup only those files that have been *modified* since the last backup. Type:

backup c: a:/m [ENTER]

We haven't modified any files at this point so the computer is unable to find a file to backup.

Restoring Files *to* the Hard Drive

If you ever really *need* your backed-up data (because you zapped something on the hard drive), you'll need to restore it from the floppy back on to the hard drive. With the disk containing the backed up files in Drive A, type:

restore a: c: [ENTER]

Then press the space bar.

The computer reports the date on which the files were backed up and the diskette number that is being restored. If it took more than one diskette to backup Drive C, the computer keeps track of which disk it is restoring.

MAKING BACKUPS OF THE TANDY 1200 HARD DISK

The Tandy 1200 will not backup files onto a diskette that already contains data. If you attempt to do so, the message:

```
Backup diskette is not blank. Use only formatted,
blank diskettes
```

will appear.

Since we will be trying two backup options in addition to doing a complete backup of the hard drive, you'll need three formatted, blank diskettes. This will prevent having to reformat your one diskette before each option.

Backing Up Files* *from* the Hard Drive

Place a formatted disk in Drive A and at the C> prompt type:

backup c:*.*a: [ENTER]

The computer instructs you to:

```
Insert diskette 01 into drive a:
then press enter
```

You already have a formatted disk in Drive A so press [ENTER] to start the backup.

The screen lists each file's name as it is being backed up from Drive C to Drive A. After all files have been backed up to the floppy disk, the computer reports:

```
Backup completed
```

Backing Up One File

Should you want the floppy backup disk to contain only one of the files currently on the hard drive, specify the file's name after the **backup** command.

Place a new formatted, blank diskette in Drive A, and type:

backup c:\print.com a: [ENTER]

Press [ENTER]. The screen displays the file name PRINT.COM and indicates:

---

* Files are the working unit of information storage. They were compared to "books on a bookshelf" in Chapter 2. All the chapters in Part Three of this book are concerned with files, so you'll become well acquainted with them.

`Backup completed`

Check the directory of Drive A. Remember that "whole bunch of files" on the first backed up diskette? This one has only the file we asked for (PRINT.COM) and a couple of additional files generated by the backup procedure.

Backing Up by Date

Whenever a file is created or modified, a date shows up on the directory. (That's what all those dates on the directory are.) A handy backup feature is the ability to back up only those files dated on or after a certain date. Suppose, for example, you wanted to backup all files that were created or modified on Drive C on or after January 1, 1984. Replace the diskette in Drive A with another formatted, blank diskette, and type:

backup c:*.* a: /d(01-01-84) `ENTER`

Press `ENTER` again after the insert-diskette instruction. When the backup is complete, check the directory of Drive A. Notice that the date for each file is later than 1-01-84.

Restoring Files *to* the Hard Drive

If you ever really *need* your backed-up *data* (because you zapped something on the hard drive), you'll need to restore it from the floppy back on to the hard drive. Insert the disk containing all the backed up files in Drive A, type:

restore a:*.* c: `ENTER`

When the insert-diskette message appears, press `ENTER` as instructed.

The computer reports the date on which the files were backed up and displays the file names as they are restored. If it took more than one diskette to backup Drive C, the computer keeps track of which disk it is restoring. When done, the message:

Restore completed

is displayed.

MAKING BACKUPS OF THE TANDY 2000 HARD DISK

Backing Up Files* *from* the Hard Drive

Place a formatted disk in Drive A and at the C> prompt type:

backup c: a: [ENTER]

The computer displays the warning:

Warning: All Files will be Deleted on Destination Diskette
Please Insert Backup Volume in directory \ into Drive A:
Strike Any Key to CONTINUE

MS-DOS is providing the opportunity to change your mind before it starts the backup procedure. It is warning that any files that may already be on Drive A's disk will be erased during the backup.

You already have a formatted disk in Drive A so press the space bar to start the backup.

The screen lists each file's name as it is being backed up from Drive C to Drive A. After all files have been backed up to the floppy disk, the computer reports:

Total number of File(s) Backed Up?   33

---

* Files are the working unit of information storage. They were compared to "books on a bookshelf" in Chapter 2. All the chapters in Part Three of this book are concerned with files, so you'll become well acquainted with them.

Backing Up One File

Should you want the floppy backup disk to contain only one of the files currently on the hard drive, specify the file's name after the **backup** command. For example, type:

backup c:print.com a: [ENTER]

The warning message is displayed again, indicating that even a single file will cause all existing files on the floppy to be erased. The screen displays the file name PRINT.COM and indicates:

```
Total number of File(s) Backed Up          1
```

Check the directory of Drive A. Remember that "whole bunch of files" that used to be on Drive A? All that remains on it is the file we asked for (PRINT.COM) and the file BACKUPID.@@@. (The computer generated this last file as part of the backup procedure.)

Backing Up by Date

Whenever a file is created or modified, a date shows up on the directory. (That's what all those dates in the directory are.) A handy backup feature is the ability to back up only those files dated on or after a certain date. Suppose, for example, you wanted to backup all files that were created or modified on Drive C on or after January 1, 1984. Type:

backup c: a:/d:01/01/84 [ENTER]

...and press [ENTER] after the warning message. When the backup is complete, check the directory of Drive A. Notice that the date for each file is later than 1-01-84.

Another variation of the command is used to backup only those files that have been *modified* since the last backup. Type:

backup c: a:/m [ENTER]

We haven't modified any files at this point so the computer is unable to find a file to backup.

Restoring Files *to* the Hard Drive

If you ever really *need* your backed-up *data* (because you zapped something on the hard drive), you'll need to restore it from the floppy back on to the hard drive. With the disk containing the backed up files in Drive A, type:

restore a: c: [ENTER]

Then press the space bar.

The computer reports the date on which the files were backed up and the diskette number that is being restored. If it took more than one diskette to backup Drive C, the computer keeps track of which disk it is restoring.

BACKING UP THE 3.2 SERIES COMPUTER HARD DRIVE

NOTE: You will need two formatted, blank diskettes.

The **backup** and **restore** commands need to be copied onto the hard drive from the Supplemental Programs diskette. Place the Supplemental Programs diskette in Drive A and type:

copy a:backup.com c: [ENTER]

Then type:

copy a:restore.com c: [ENTER]

Backing Up Files* *from* the Hard Drive

Place a formatted disk in Drive A and at the ⊏⟩ prompt, type:

---

* A file is the working unit of information storage. They were compared to "books on the bookshelf" in Chapter 2. All the chapters in Part Three of this book are concerned with files, so you'll become well acquainted with them.

backup c: a: [ENTER]

The computer displays:

```
Insert backup diskette 01 in drive A:
```

followed by the warning:

```
Warning! File in the target drive
A:\ root directory will be erased
Strike any key when ready
```

MS-DOS is providing an opportunity to change your mind before it starts the backup procedure. It is warning that any files that may already be on Drive A's disk will be erased during the backup.

You already have a formatted disk in Drive A so press [ENTER] to start the backup.

The screen displays:

```
***Backing up files to drive A: ***
Diskette Number: 01
```

Each file's name is listed as it is being backed up from Drive C to Drive A. When the first disk is full, the computer instructs:

```
Insert backup diskette 02 in Drive A:
```

and displays the same warning message. Replace the full disk with a second formatted, blank disk and press [ENTER]. After all files have been backed up to the floppy disk, the C> returns.

Backing Up One File

Should you want the floppy backup disk to contain only one of the files currently on the hard drive, specify the file's name after the **backup** command. For example, with that second disk still in Drive A, type:

backup c:print.com a: ENTER

The warning message is displayed again, indicating that even a single file will cause all existing files on the floppy to be erased. After PRINT.COM has been backed up to Drive A, the C> prompt returns.

Check the directory of Drive A. Remember that "whole bunch of files" that used to be on Drive A? All that remains on it is the file we asked for (PRINT.COM) and the file BACKUPID.@@@. (The computer generated that last file as part of the backup procedure.)

Adding a File to the Backup Disk

It is possible to add individual files to the backup floppy without erasing everything on it. This time let's backup the file SORT.EXE without losing the PRINT.COM file. Type:

backup c:sort.exe a:/a ENTER

And we are asked to:

```
Insert last backup diskette in drive A:
Strike any key when ready
```

MS-DOS is asking us to be certain the disk in Drive A is the last backup disk. This is due to the /a option, which tells **backup** to add the file (SORT.EXE) to files already backed up. Press ENTER to continue.

Check the Drive A directory again. Adding the /a at the end of the **backup** command caused MS-DOS to *copy* SORT.EXE from Drive C to Drive A and add it to what was already on that disk.

Backing Up by Date

Whenever a file is created or modified, a date shows up on the directory. (That's what all those dates in the directory are.) A handy backup feature is the ability to back up only those files dated on or after a certain date. Suppose, for example, you wanted to backup all files that were created or modified on Drive C on or after March 15, 1986. Type:

backup c: a:/d:03-15-86 [ENTER]

...and press [ENTER] after the warning message. When the backup is complete, check the directory of Drive A. Notice that the date for each file is later than 3-15-86. (The files actually backed up will vary depending on the computer.)

Another variation of the command is used to backup only those files that have been *modified* since the last backup. Type:

backup c: a:/m [ENTER]

We haven't modified any files at this point so the computer is unable to find a file to backup.

Restoring Files *to* the Hard Drive

If you ever really *need* your backed-up data (because you zapped something on the hard drive), you'll need to restore it from the floppy back on to the hard drive. With the disk containing the backed up files in Drive A, type:

restore a: c: [ENTER]

That \ puts all the data into the root directory of Drive C. You can learn more about that in **Volume 2, MS-DOS Advanced Applications**.

and press the space bar. The computer then instructs:

```
Insert backup diskette 01 in drive A:
Strike any key when ready
```

If a backup required more than one disk to store the files from Drive C, the computer is telling us to insert the first one. In our situation, one disk was enough, so tap the space bar.

The computer reports the date on which the files were backed up and the diskette number that is being restored. If it took more than one diskette to backup Drive C, the computer informs us when to insert the next disk.

* The **backup** command is used to *copy* data from the hard drive to a floppy.
* The **restore** command is used to move backed-up data from a floppy to the hard drive.

MAKING BACKUPS OF THE TANDY 1000 HARD DRIVE (DOS 2.11)

1. Insert the Hard Disk Utilities diskette in Drive A.
2. Type **copy a:backup.exe c:** [ENTER] to copy the **backup** command onto the hard drive.
3. Type **copy a:restore.exe c:** [ENTER] to copy the **restore** command onto the hard drive.
4. Replace the Hard Disk Utilities disk with a formatted, blank diskette.
5. To backup all the files from the hard disk to a floppy, type **backup c: a:** [ENTER] at the C> prompt.
6. After the warning display comes up, press [ENTER].

* To backup one file (named FILENAME) from the hard drive to a floppy, type **backup c:filename a:** [ENTER] at the C> prompt.
* To add a file (named FILENAME) to the floppy backup disk, type **backup c:filename a:/a** [ENTER] at the C> prompt.
* To backup by date, type **backup c: a:/d:***mm/dd/yy* [ENTER] at the C> prompt. (*mm* = month, *dd* = day, *yy* = year)
* To backup only modified files, type **backup c: a:/m** [ENTER].

To restore files from the floppy backup disk to the hard drive:
1. Insert diskette with backup in Drive A.
2. Type **restore a: c:** [ENTER].
3. Press [ENTER].

MAKING BACKUPS OF THE TANDY 1200 HARD DRIVE

* A *blank*, formatted diskette must be used each time a backup--whether of one or all files--is made.

1. Insert a formatted, blank diskette in Drive A.
2. At the C> prompt, type **backup c:*.*a:** [ENTER].
3. Press [ENTER].

* To backup one file (named FILENAME) from the hard drive to a floppy, type **backup c:\filename a:** [ENTER].
* To backup by date, type **backup c:*.* a: /d(mm-dd-yy)** [ENTER]. (*mm* = month, *dd* = day, *yy* = year)

To restore files from the floppy backup disk to the hard drive:
1. Insert diskette with backup in Drive A.
2. Type **restore a:*.* c:** [ENTER].
3. Press [ENTER] again.

MAKING BACKUPS OF THE TANDY 2000 HARD DRIVE
1. Insert a formatted floppy disk in Drive A.
2. At the C> prompt, type **backup c: a:** [ENTER].
3. After the warning is displayed, press space bar.

* To backup one file (named FILENAME) from the hard drive to a floppy, type **backup c:filename a:** [ENTER] at the C> prompt.
* To backup by date, type **backup c: a:/d:*mm/dd/yy*** [ENTER] at the C> prompt. (*mm* = month, *dd* = day, *yy* = year)
* To backup only modified files, type **backup c: a:/m** [ENTER].

To restore files from the floppy backup disk to the hard drive:
1. Insert diskette with backup in Drive A.
2. Type **restore a: c:** [ENTER].
3. Press [ENTER].

BACKING UP THE 3.2 SERIES COMPUTER HARD DRIVE
1. Insert the Supplemental Programs diskette in Drive A.
2. Type **copy a:backup.com c:** [ENTER] to copy the **backup** command onto the hard drive.
3. Type **copy a:restore.com c:** [ENTER] to copy the **restore** command onto the hard drive.
4. Replace the Supplemental Programs disk with a formatted, blank diskette.
5. To backup all the files from the hard disk to a floppy, type **backup c: a:** [ENTER] at the C> prompt.
6. After the warning display comes up, press [ENTER].

* To backup one file (named FILENAME) from the hard drive to a floppy, type **backup c:filename a:** [ENTER] at the C> prompt.
* To add a file (named FILENAME) to the floppy backup disk, type **backup c:filename a:/a** [ENTER] at the C> prompt.
* To backup by date, type **backup c: a:/d:*mm-dd-yy*** [ENTER] at the C> prompt. (*mm* = month, *dd* = day, *yy* = year)
* To backup only modified files, type **backup c: a:/m** [ENTER].

To restore files from the floppy backup disk to the hard drive:

1. Insert diskette with backup in Drive A.
2. Type **restore a: c:** ENTER .
3. Press space bar.

CHAPTER 13

Comparing Two Diskettes

Backup copies of diskettes are a way of life with computers. We've already suggested you use a copy of the MS-DOS diskette for everyday use, and when you begin saving your own data "on-disk," the practice of keeping backup copies will save you a lot of grief due to lost or damaged diskettes. One of the drawbacks of having copies, however, is that it can get confusing if you forget which is the latest copy. Was a copy made after the last minor change? Is this an exact copy? Has someone made changes you're not aware of?

The only certain way is to compare the two disks in question, a byte at a time. There is a command to do this for the 1000s/1200/3000s, and another command for the 2000 with two floppy disk drives. Read the section below that applies to your computer.

TANDY 1000s, 1200 AND 3000s

Put the original MS-DOS disk back in Drive A and the copy of it in Drive B. Type:

diskcomp a: b: [ENTER]

One-Drive Systems
Simply type **diskcomp a:** [ENTER]. As usual, you will be prompted when it's time to swap disks.

MS-DOS asks you to insert the disks you want compared:

```
Insert first diskette in drive A:
Strike any key when ready
```

You've done that, so tap the space bar and you're asked to:

```
Insert second diskette in drive B:
Strike any key when ready
```

...which you've also done. Tap the space bar again.

Press any key. MS-DOS gears up for the comparison, and delivers the following message:

```
Comparing 9 sectors per track, 2 side(s)*
```

When the comparison is finished, MS-DOS reports that:

```
Diskettes compare ok
```

...and offers to:

```
Compare more diskettes (Y/N)?
```

---

* Every computer covered by this book, except those with 1.2M drives, uses "9-sector" tracks. (The 1.2M disks use "15-sector" tracks.) All that means is that the concentric rings, or tracks, laid down on the diskette during formatting are further divided into individual segments called sectors. It helps the computer find things, but it's nothing that you, the operator, should ever have to worry about. Older versions of MS-DOS used 8-sector tracks, so, should you ever find yourself comparing two of these older disks, the command to use is **diskcomp/8**. Older versions also used single-sided diskettes, and to compare two of them, the command is **diskcomp/1**. To compare single-sided, 8 sector disks, use **diskcomp/8/1**.

Press $\boxed{Y}$ and when prompted to do so, insert the formatted disk you named SAMPLE_DISK into Drive A. Put a blank, unnamed formatted disk in Drive B (or prepare to swap them back and forth in Drive A if you have a single drive). The two disks you are comparing this time should be identical with the exception of the name, or "Volume Label". Let's see what happens.

A few seconds into the operation a new message appears:

```
Compare error(s) on
Track 0, Side 0

Compare error(s) on
Track 0, Side 1
```

MS-DOS is saying it found a "compare error" on Track 0, Side 0, and another one on Track 0, Side 1. Computer engineers like to use "0" for the first item on a list. The 40 tracks on a disk are numbered 0 through 39 (0 to 79 on the 2000 and 3000s for a total of 80), and the two sides are 0 and 1.

Looks like the Volume Label, SAMPLE_DISK, is recorded on the first track on each side of the disk. This causes the compare error. Any compare errors found by MS-DOS indicate that the disks are not identical, and that's the purpose of the **diskcomp** command.

TANDY 2000 (with two floppy disk drives)

The 2000 provides a couple of extra features. In addition to simply comparing two disks, it will make a copy of a disk and then compare it to the original. It will also format a new disk, use it to make a copy of the original, then compare the two.

We'll be using the MS-DOS diskette as a sample "source" disk in this chapter, but you can replace it with any disk you'd like to compare or duplicate when prompted on the screen to do so.

To make a simple comparison on the 2000, place the original MS-DOS diskette in Drive A and the copy of it in Drive B and type:

compdupe ENTER

A copyright notice appears on the screen, along with some information about different *variations* of compdupes (which we'll come back to shortly) and an instruction to press the space bar when ready. Compdupe will also instruct you to insert source and destination disks, in the event you don't want to use the one(s) currently in the drive(s). When ready, press the space bar.

The computer displays a line of dashes to represent each track on the disks. As each track passes the comparison test, the dash is changed to a dot.

Watch the dash closely as the comparison is made. Notice that an asterisk (*) appears before the dash is replaced with a dot. The asterisk means that the computer compared the data on that track and found no errors. It is one of several symbols used in the comparison. Had the computer found a difference between the two disks, the dash would be replaced with the letter C.

When the comparison is finished, MS-DOS asks:

AGAIN (Y/N):

Press Y and when prompted to do so, insert the formatted disk you named SAMPLE_DISK into Drive A. Put a blank, unnamed formatted disk in Drive B (or prepare to swap them back and forth in Drive A if you have a single drive). The two disks you'll be comparing this time should be identical with the exception of the name, or Volume Label. Press the space bar and watch the screen.

Notice that the first dash is changed to an asterisk followed by the letter C. As soon as the first difference is encountered, MS-DOS stops the comparison and announces:

```
Disks do not compare

AGAIN (Y/N):
```

Answer by pressing ☐N☐.

Looks like the name, SAMPLE_DISK, is recorded on the very first track of the disk. Any comparison errors found by MS-DOS indicate that the disks are not identical, and that's the purpose of the **compdupe** command.

Duplicating Disks (2000 with two floppy disk drives only)

In Chapter 7 you learned how to format a disk and later you used a formatted disk to make a copy of the master diskette. With the **compdupe** command we have the options of formatting, duplicating and comparing two diskettes all in one step by typing a slight variation of the **compdupe** command. (This is the first of those "different kinds of compdupes" we said we'd come back to.)

Place the MS-DOS disk in Drive A and a blank *unformatted* disk in Drive B and type:

compdupe /d ☐ENTER☐

When the message appears, press the space bar. This time the computer reads the data on Drive A and reports a successful read by displaying an asterisk. It then formats that track on the disk in Drive B, copies the data onto it and compares what it copied with the original. If no errors occurred, the asterisk is replaced with a dot and the computer moves on to the next track.

If the computer has a problem formatting one of the tracks in the new disk, the dash for that track will be replaced with the letter F. Another possible error can occur when the computer is unable to write the data to the formatted track. Should this occur, the dash is replaced with the letter D. If an error does occur with the new diskette during the duplicating process, bulk erase the diskette (with a magnetic bulk eraser, available at most Radio Shack stores), and try again, or start over with another new disk.

Once the entire disk is copied without errors, the computer reports:

```
Disks duplicated with no errors

AGAIN (Y/N):
```

Duplicating Formatted Disks (2000 with two floppy disk drives only)

When you already have formatted blank disks available, the format step can be skipped in the **compdupe**. Leave the MS-DOS disk in Drive A, and insert a blank *formatted* diskette in Drive B. (Single-drive users have a blank formatted disk ready for swapping with the MS-DOS disk when prompted to do so.)

Answer the AGAIN (Y/N) question with an N then type:

compdupe /d /s ENTER

The /d tells the computer to duplicate the disk before comparing and the /s tells it to skip the format routine.

By skipping the format routine the duplication procedure takes a little less time than it did before--it takes time to format each track.

SUMMARY

* Diskette sectors are numbered 0-9 or on 1.2M high capacity disks, 0-14.
* The 40 tracks on a diskette are number 0-39 (0-79 for the 80 tracks on the 2000 and 3000s).

TANDY 1000s, 1200 AND 3000s

* Type **diskcomp a: b:** to compare two diskettes (**diskcomp a:** for single-drive systems).
* If differences are found, MS-DOS reports Compare error(s).
* Sides of a diskette are called 0 and 1

TANDY 2000 (with two floppy disk drives)

* Type **compdupe** to compare two disks.
* Type **compdupe** **/d** to format, duplicate and compare two disks.
* Type **compdupe** **/d** **/s** to duplicate (skip formatting) and compare two disks.

CHAPTER 14

Checking the Disk

Another Way to Look at a Disk

As you know, the **dir** command produces a list of all the files on a particular disk, along with some other useful information. The **chkdsk** (check disk) command provides a quick rundown of the memory situation--what the space on the disk is being used for, how many bytes are available, and how much of the computer's own RAM memory is currently being used. In multiple-drive systems, the disk in any drive can be checked. Just specify the drive after giving the command. With the MS-DOS disk in Drive A, type:

chkdsk a: `ENTER` *

MS-DOS responds with a short report:

```
362496 bytes total disk space
 23552 bytes in 2 hidden files
299008 bytes in 32 user files
 39936 bytes available on disk

114688 bytes total memory
 89520 bytes free
```

---

* This also works with the hard disk. Type **chkdsk c:** `ENTER`

Your numbers may vary, of course, depending upon the computer and amount of memory you are using. This is a handy little report, one that you should run from time to time when you think you might be getting low on memory or disk space. The "hidden files" referred to are MS-DOS's own *system* files-- those that actually control MS-DOS. Since they don't show up on the directory, they're called hidden files. (In case you're curious, the names of the 2.11 Series hidden files are IO.SYS and MSDOS.SYS. For the 3.2 Series, they're IBMBIO.COM and IBMDOS.COM.)

The "user files" listed are the other programs that come with MS-DOS--the ones accessed by the "external" commands like **format** and **diskcopy**. If you were to save any of your own files on this disk, they would be included under "user files."

The "total memory" number refers to the computer's RAM. If your machine advertises 256K, you actually have 262,144 bytes total RAM available. Because of the amount of RAM being used by MS-DOS, the computer (in the above example) can spare a little over 220 kilobytes for your own work before you need to transfer some of it onto a disk and "clean house" to make room for more data.

The **chkdsk** command can also perform several other tricks. In the event errors are encountered during the check, they will be flagged, or in some cases, can be corrected. Since the MS-DOS disk (hopefully) has no errors resulting from improper saving, we won't be able to demonstrate it now, but the command to fix errors is **chkdsk/f**. Before the short report (above) appears, any necessary error messages will be displayed, and any errors MS-DOS can fix will be automatically taken care of. Remember this for later when something doesn't seem to be acting right. There may be an error in a file that **chkdsk/f** can fix.

An even more detailed check can be made with a variation of the command. **chkdsk/v** not only checks and repairs, it provides detailed messages about any errors it finds.

There is one other variation of **chkdsk**. We haven't talked much about files yet, but you have seen the names of the ones on the MS-DOS disk, and you know what files are--the major unit in which information is stored on the disk; the "book" on the bookshelf.

If a file is big enough to require more than one segment to hold it, MS-DOS normally breaks it into adjacent segments. As files are added, they are lined up on the tracks, neat as you please. But when a file you no longer need is deleted, the remaining files don't move together. The deleted file just leaves a hole. Eventually, you could end up with files scattered all over the surface of the disk, with numerous vacant spots in between.

MS-DOS, however, doesn't believe in wasting space, so when asked to save a long file, it's likely to distribute pieces of it among several of these small vacancies. This disjointing of a file into non-contiguous areas of the disk has no effect on you or your work, except that the computer may take a little longer to load a file into RAM since it has to go on a scavenger hunt for the pieces.

If you like things tidy and you're concerned about a very important file being chopped up into too many parts (or if it seems to be taking a long time to load), you can check to see if the file is contiguous by using the **chkdsk** command. Add to the command the full name of the file in question. Let's pick one from the MS-DOS directory--say, PRINT.COM (the period separates the file name from its extension--we'll get into all that later). Type the command and the file name:

chkdsk print.com [ENTER]

The same report appears, followed by the message:

```
All specified file(s) are contiguous,
```

Should the file in which you're interested be fragmented, MS-DOS will say so, and you can move it to a fresh disk where there is room to keep it all together. (We'll learn how to move a file from one disk to another in Chapter 18.)

SUMMARY

* Type **chkdsk a:** to check the disk in Drive A.
* To check for and repair errors on Drive A, type **chkdsk/f a:**.
* To check, repair and obtain detailed error messages, type **chkdsk/v a:**.
* When files are deleted, new files are broken up and stored in the vacant spaces created by deleting files. Type **chkdsk** and the file name to determine if a file is contiguous.

CHAPTER 15

Review of Part Two

Part Two has been an introduction to the MS-DOS commands that are used to prepare and handle your diskettes. Floppy disks used by the Tandy 1000 Series, 1200, and 3000 HL can store approximately 120 pages of text. Tandy 2000 disks and 3-1/2" diskettes hold approximately 240 pages, whereas the Tandy 3000 high capacity disks hold approximately 400 pages. A 10 megabyte hard drive holds about 3000 pages, 20 meg. holds 6000, and so on.

If your computer has 128K of built-in (RAM) memory, you can have up to approximately 38 pages loaded and active at any one time. Double that number for 256K and so on.

Each disk must be *formatted* before it can be used to store information, and copies or *backups* of all important disks should be kept for security.

Both floppy and hard drive disks need to be protected from accidental erasures or changes. All floppies can be protected with write protect tabs. The 3-1/2" diskettes have write-protect locking mechanisms.

PCMAKER.COM can be used to format 360K diskettes in the 2000's 720K drive.

On the Tandy 1200, a *blank,* formatted diskette must be used each time a backup is made.

Common Commands

backup c: a: (not Tandy 1000 EX and 1200) copies files from the hard drive (Drive C) to Drive A.

backup c: a:/d:01/01/87 (not Tandy 1000 EX and 1200) backs up all files dated Jan. 1, 1987 or later from Drive C to Drive A. Tandy 3000 uses the format **backup c: a:/d:01-01-87**.

backup c: a:/m (not Tandy 1000 EX and 1200) copies only those files that have been modified since the last backup from Drive C to A.

backup c:somefile a: (not Tandy 1000 EX and 1200) backs up only the file named SOMEFILE from Drive C to Drive A. Any other files already on Drive A will be erased.

chkdsk followed by a file name determines if the file is contiguous or distributed over disk in spaces left by cancelled files.

chkdsk a: checks the disk in Drive A for errors.

chkdsk/f a: checks the disk in Drive A and repairs some errors.

chkdsk/v a: checks the disk in Drive A, repairs errors and displays error messages.

copy a:*.* c: (not Tandy 1000 EX) copies all the Drive A files to hard disk, Drive C. (This command must be used in place of **diskcopy** to make copies between 5-1/4" and 3-1/2" diskettes.)

diskcomp a: b: (not Tandy 2000) compares the disk in Drive A to the one in Drive B.

diskcopy a: b: copies the disk in Drive A to a blank, formatted disk in Drive B.

format b: formats the diskette in Drive B. Other drives may be specified.

format/v b: provides opportunity to name diskette in Drive B. (On the 3.2 Series computers, it's **format b:/v**.)

label a: (version 3.1 and higher) provides opportunity to add, change, or delete volume label of diskette in Drive A.

restore a: c: (Tandy 1000 and 2000 only) restores all files from Drive A to Drive C. Hard disk is not erased, but any files on the hard disk with the same name as on the floppy will be written over.

vol a: displays the name of the diskette in Drive A.

TANDY 1000, 1000 SX, AND 3000 SERIES

backup c:somefile a:/a copies only the file named SOMEFILE from Drive C and *adds* it to Drive A. Does not erase other files from Drive A.

fdisk begins initialization of the hard drive.

format a:/4 (Tandy 3000) formats a 360K diskette in a 1.2M drive.

hsect begins formatting the hard drive.

TANDY 1000 ONLY

copy a:backup.exe c: copies the **backup** command from the Hard Disk Utilities disk to the hard drive.

copy a:restore.exe c: copies the **restore** command from the Hard Disk Utilities disk to the hard drive.

hformat c: /s/v/b prepares the hard disk to receive MS-DOS.

3.2 SERIES COMPUTERS ONLY

copy a:backup.com c: copies the **backup** command from the Supplemental Programs disk to the hard drive.

copy a:restore.com c: copies the **restore** command from the Supplemental Programs disk to the hard drive.

format c:/s/v prepares the hard disk to receive MS-DOS.

restore a: c: restores all files from Drive A to Drive C. Hard disk is not erased, but any files on the hard disk with the same name as on the floppy will be written over.

TANDY 1200 ONLY

backup c:*.* a: copies all files from the hard drive (Drive C) to Drive A.

backup c:*.* a: /d(01-01-84) copies all files dated Jan. 1, 1984 or later from Drive C to Drive A.

backup c:\somefile a: copies only the file named SOMEFILE from Drive C to Drive A.

format c: /s/f prepares the hard disk to receive MS-DOS.

llfdfmt begins formatting the hard drive.

part displays the Partition Menu and begins phase two of the format procedure.

restore a:*.* c: copies all files from Drive A to Drive C.

TANDY 2000 ONLY

compdupe (2 floppy disk drives only) compares the disk in Drive A to the one in Drive B.

compdupe /d (2 floppy disk drives only) formats the disk in Drive B, uses it to make a copy of the disk in Drive A, then compares the two.

compdupe /d /s (2 floppy disk drives only) copies the disk in Drive A onto the disk in Drive B, but skips the formatting step. A formatted disk must be inserted in Drive B. If the disk in Drive B contains data, it will be written over.

confighd begins formatting the hard drive.

P A R T   3

Using MS-DOS to manage your files

CHAPTER 16

What's a File?

What's a File?

We've suggested that a file on a disk could be considered roughly equivalent to a book on a bookshelf or, perhaps, as a file in a filing cabinet. In any case, it is the basic unit of storage for computer data. Just as there are books for different purposes--books for reading, books for reference and so on--there are also disk files for different purposes. We could go into great detail about the subtle differences among file types, but for now, all you need to know is that there are the three primary types of files: *program files*, *data files* and *system files*.

Program Files

Program files make the computer do something. For example, the FORMAT file on the MS-DOS disk contains the instructions to the computer which cause it to format a disk. The program is started with the command **format**.

Most of the files on the MS-DOS disk are programs, and their extensions are either .COM for command or .EXE for executable. All the commands we refer to as "external" commands are program files. When you later add an application program, such as a word processor or a spreadsheet, it will be made up, in part, of program files.

Data Files

Data files are the kind you fill with your own data--letters written using a word processor, budgets and forecasts using a spreadsheet, and so on. Data files are generally given the extensions .DAT (data) or .TXT (text). *Generally speaking*, data files are stored in a format which you can read, and program files are stored in a format readable only by the machine ("machine language").

System Files

Files which have the .SYS extension are the heart of MS-DOS. These files contain the information MS-DOS needs to communicate with the computer. While .COM and .EXE *program files* such as FORMAT.COM and DISK-COPY.COM could be considered external "accessories" to MS-DOS, the *system files* are the "engine" and "transmission" that make the whole thing go. In addition to all their behind-the-scenes work, the system files also contain the internal commands, like **dir** and **copy**. It is because the system files remain in memory at all times that these internal commands work immediately, without the necessity of being read from the disk. Once MS-DOS has been loaded, even if you remove the MS-DOS disk, the system files remain in memory to keep things running.

Although the above descriptions cover the file types you will most commonly use, you should also be aware of the following:

Batch Files

The number of commands available make MS-DOS a very powerful system. It is possible to make it even more powerful, however, by chaining several commands together, saving them in a special "batch" file and activating it with a single command. As you learn more commands, you'll begin to see some interesting possibilities for this technique, and in Volume 2 we'll discuss building batch files in detail.

BASIC Files

One of the major programs that comes with MS-DOS is BASIC. BASIC, in case you aren't really sure, is a "language," a program designed to allow you to write your own programs. Programs you create using BASIC will have the extension .BAS. We'll do a little program writing in the next chapter.

PROGRAM FILES

Programs, such as FORMAT.COM and DISKCOPY.COM., that cause the computer to perform useful tasks. Usually written in machine language and loaded by single-word commands: (**format, chkdsk, backup, label, diskcomp, diskcopy**). Extensions: .COM, .EXE.

Programs which you buy, word processors and spreadsheet, for example, also use the .COM and .EXE extension.

DATA FILES

Information or text created by user. Usually written in plain English. Examples: documents created using word processors or lists of figures created using spreadsheet programs. Extensions: .TXT, .DAT.

SYSTEM FILES

The built-in parts of MS-DOS. Control such details as screen layouts, keyboard functions and general file-handling procedures. Also operate "internal" commands, such as **dir, date, time, copy** and **cls**. Extension: .SYS.

OTHERS

1. Batch files: Sequences of commands stored in a file, designed to execute a complex chain of events with a single command. Extension: .BAT.

2. BASIC files: User-created programs written and executed using the BASIC programming language. Extension: .BAS.

CHAPTER 17

Creating a Sample File Using BASIC

BASIC Programming Language

One of the "accessory" programs that comes with MS-DOS is the BASIC programming language. We're going to give you just a taste of BASIC here because it's a handy tool for creating some sample files to put on one of your formatted data diskettes. Once you have some files to work with, we can demonstrate more of MS-DOS's capabilities.

BASIC programming, by the way, can be very useful and is a lot of fun. If you are interested in learning it, I recommend, as a start-to-finish tutorial course, **Learning BASIC for Tandy Computers** (Radio Shack Cat. No. 25-1500). As a reference book, there is no substitute for **The BASIC Handbook, 3rd Edition** (available at better bookstores worldwide). I wrote both of them, and both are published by CompuSoft Publishing.

Loading BASIC

BASIC itself is a program file, and it can be activated by simply typing its name. With the MS-DOS disk in Drive A, a formatted diskette in Drive B and the system prompt on the screen, type:

BASIC [ENTER]

One-Drive Systems
After typing **basic**, remove the MS-DOS disk and insert a blank formatted diskette.

Tandy 2000
Users with the High-Resolution Graphics option will see a blank screen and
the keyboard will appear "frozen" after loading BASIC. If this is your case,
press the Reset switch and watch the light on the [NUM LOCK] or [CAPS] key.
The light will go out as soon as Reset is pressed. After a couple seconds,
the light will flash on and off. When this happens, immediately tap the
[F12] key. The computer is fussy about when [F12] must be pressed, so keep
trying until you are successful then type:

BASIC [ENTER]

MS-DOS gives you a clue that you've just loaded a major program by pre-
senting a copyright notice. At the top of your screen you will see the name
of the program: GW-BASIC (or Model 2000 BASIC), a version number and
some copyright and licensing information. Under that, there is a memory
report similar to:

60875 Bytes free (Your number may vary.)

BASIC allows you to use only a fixed block of memory, in this example,
about 60k, even though the computer is equipped with more RAM. Advanced
users can access more memory, but for our purposes, 60k is more than
enough.

Under the memory notice is BASIC's own prompt:

Ok

This prompt has the same purpose as the MS-DOS system prompt. It means
the program is not busy. It's Ok for you to go ahead and do something. The
Ok prompt also serves to remind you that you are in BASIC, not at MS-DOS
command level.

At the bottom of the screen there is now a row of numbers, each followed
by a word. The first is LIST, the second is RUN and so on. These represent
the *function keys*, the keys labeled [F1] through [F12] (through [F10] on the
1200 and 3000s). Only ten of the twelve keys are being used. The function
keys are nothing more than shortcut keys. They do in one keystroke what

would take three or four to do "manually." We'll only use a couple of them for our purposes. You'll see how they work in a moment.

Because BASIC is a language, or a "programmer's program," we can use it to create programs of our own. Those you create in this chapter will give you a small taste of what a BASIC program can do and will give you some sample files to play with. This chapter will not be a lesson in BASIC; we'll simply walk you through a few short programs.

Line Numbers

Every line in a BASIC program tells the computer, in a language it understands, to do something. Therefore, each line must be a distinctly numbered instruction. It is customary to number BASIC lines by tens--10, 20, 30 etc.

Sample Program 1 - Math Calculation

Math is one of the things a computer does best, so our first program will do a little math problem. We'll give the computer a few numbers, then ask it to add and subtract them. BASIC will accept either upper- or lowercase, but when you're finished typing, it converts everything (except whatever may be enclosed in quotes) to uppercase. Just to make things simpler, press the CAPS key, and type the programs in uppercase.

At the OK prompt, type your first numbered line:

10 REM MATH CALCULATION ENTER

REM in BASIC means *remark*. A REM line does not cause the computer to do anything. It's just there as a note. You can stick a REM line anywhere in a program. Finish typing in the following program, pressing ENTER at the end of each line:

```
20 A = 1000
30 B = 750
40 C = 25
50 PRINT A-B + C
```

When a computer runs a BASIC program, it starts at the first line and works its way down through each successive line. When this little program is run, it will ignore the first line, the REM line, then observe that A = 1000, that B = 750 and that C = 25. These are just arbitrary values we chose for the real work which is in line 50. Line 50 tells the computer to print (on the screen) the sum of 1000-750 + 25.

All it takes to run a BASIC program is typing the word **RUN** [ENTER], but notice that there is a function key that even does that for you. Press the [F2] key. [F2] automatically "types" **RUN** [ENTER], and almost immediately, the answer to the math problem appears.

```
RUN
 275
OK
```

You have just written and run a computer program. You put in some numbers, and the computer calculated them and displayed the answer you requested. In a very simple way, this program demonstrates what every computer program does: it gives the computer instructions. The computer goes through them, one at a time, and performs the tasks as instructed. Play with the program a little. Change line 40 to **C = 50**. All that's required to change a BASIC program line is to retype that line. No need to type the whole program over.* Type:

40 C = 50 [ENTER]

...and press [F2] to run the program again. Predictably, a change in the information causes a change in the answer, which is now 300.

To see your program in its revised form, it is necessary to *list* it, and if you refer to the bottom of the screen, you'll see that function key [F1] accomplishes this task. Press [F1] [ENTER].

---

*If you already know something about BASIC, you know there are ways to edit program lines without retyping the whole line. This way is simple, however, and good enough for our purpose.

There's the program again, with its new line 40. Change any of the lines you wish, including the equation in line 50. The sign for "divided by" in BASIC is the /, and for "multiplied by," use *. You can even use parentheses, just like you do on paper. Whatever numbers you use in whatever equation you create, BASIC will give you the answer when you press [F2] to *run*.

When you're finished experimenting with this sample program, *save* it onto the formatted data disk by pressing the **SAVE"** function key [F4] and typing the designator of the drive holding your formatted data diskette, which is B: in a two-drive system, or A: in a one-drive system, or C: for a hard drive.

SAVE"B:MATH" [ENTER]

The " separating the command SAVE from the name is required by BASIC, so the function key puts it in automatically. The " after the name is good programming practice, so be sure to type it in.

Notice that when you assign a file name to a certain drive, the drive designation goes *before* the name. This rule applies to all MS-DOS files, not just BASIC files.

The disk spins when you press [ENTER], and your first file is saved on the new disk. Before we leave BASIC to look at the directory (and while we're on a roll...), let's add a couple more.

Clearing the Memory

One thing about BASIC, it believes everything it sees. If you have one program loaded (like MATH) and you type in another program, BASIC will try to run them both and become confused. Whenever you're finished working with one BASIC program, make sure it's been saved to disk, then type:

NEW [ENTER]

This clears out whatever program is in memory so that any new program won't conflict with the old. Now type this second sample program (remember to [ENTER] at the end of each line):

Sample Program 2 · Greeting

```
10 REM GREETING
20 INPUT "WHAT IS YOUR NAME";A$
30 PRINT "HELLO THERE, ";A$
```

Don't worry too much about how the program works, just try to type it accurately. Watch those quotation marks (") and semi-colons (;) and the comma and space after HELLO THERE.

Press [F2] to run the program, and when asked your name, type it in and press [ENTER]. Once the computer has said hello to you and returned the Ok prompt, save the program as B:GREETING with the [F4] key.

You now have a program that does a math problem and one that talks to you. How about one more that does something useful? After GREETING is saved, type **NEW** to clear the memory and **CLS** (remember **CLS**?) to clear the clutter off the screen, then type this program:

Sample Program 3 · Celsius to Fahrenheit Conversion

```
10 REM CELSIUS TO FAHRENHEIT CONVERSION
20 INPUT "WHAT IS THE TEMPERATURE IN DEGREES (C)";C
30 F=(9/5)*C+32
40 PRINT C;"DEGREES (C) =";F;"DEGREES (F)."
50 PRINT : GOTO 20
```

When you run this program, it will ask you for a Celsius temperature. Type any number (try 25) and [ENTER]. The Fahrenheit equivalent of the temperature you typed will instantly appear, and you'll be asked for the next temperature you wish to have converted. To stop the program and return to the Ok prompt, press the [CTRL] and [BREAK] keys. Use the name B:CONVERT to save this program.

Loading a BASIC Program from the Disk

There's another function key you may be wondering about--the [F3] "Load" key. Yes, it is used for loading BASIC programs from disk back into memory. Clear the memory with **NEW** and the screen with **CLS**, then press [F3] and type the name of one of your new files; for example:

[F3] **B:GREETING"** [ENTER]

All you will see is the ΟK prompt, but the program is indeed loaded. To see it, press [F1] [ENTER] (to list). To run it, press [F2].

Getting Back to MS-DOS

With three sample programs under your belt, it's time to end this brief excursion into BASIC and return to MS-DOS. Type:

SYSTEM [ENTER]

One-Drive Systems
You will have to put the MS-DOS disk back in Drive A to reload MS-DOS or to use any other "external" command, such as **diskcopy** or **format**.

SUMMARY

* The BASIC programming language is a program that comes with MS-DOS.
* Load BASIC by typing **BASIC** [ENTER].
* List a BASIC program by typing **LIST** [ENTER] or by pressing [F1] [ENTER].
* Run a BASIC program by typing **RUN** [ENTER] or by pressing [F2].
* Load a BASIC program by typing **LOAD"** or by pressing [F3]. Then type the name of the file you wish to load and press [ENTER].
* Save a BASIC program by typing **SAVE"** or by pressing [F4]. Then type the name under which you wish to save the file and [ENTER]. (The name may include the drive designation.)
* To clear memory of the currently-loaded BASIC file(s) to prepare for another, type **NEW** [ENTER].
* Clear the screen by typing **CLS** [ENTER].
* When specifying a drive for a file name, the drive designation goes at the beginning of the name. Example: B:MATH.
* To exit BASIC and return to MS-DOS, type **SYSTEM** [ENTER].

Copying Files

Now that you have some sample .BAS files on your data disk, we can begin using some of MS-DOS's file handling features.

File handling? Most of your computer work will probably be with application programs--a word processor, a spreadsheet, a database or a programming language. Every application stores information in the form of files, and most have some file handling capabilities of their own. It's often more convenient, however, to use the MS-DOS operating system to copy files or compare them or delete them. When you let MS-DOS do the job, you can work on files from several different applications at the same time, look at the directories, rearrange files, then go right back to the directory to check your work.

Speaking of directories, let's check the data disk to see if those new BASIC program files made it. Be sure the data disk is in Drive B and the system prompt is on the screen, then type **dir b:**

One-Drive Systems
Put the data disk in the only drive and type **dir**.

```
Volume in drive B is SAMPLE_DISK
Directory of  B:\
```

```
MATH      BAS       68      9-25-85    10:15a
GREETING BAS       57      9-25-85    10:20a
CONVERT  BAS      165      9-25-85    10:30a
         3 File(s)      359424 bytes free

A>
```

There they are--all the new files. BASIC automatically added the BAS extension to them for you, which means that from now on, you'll have to refer
to them by their full names, including the **.BAS**. The period does not show
up on the directory, but you must include it whenever you type the file name
so that MS-DOS will know you intend the extension to be just that, an extension, and not part of the actual name. (The 2000 and 3000s store files differently, so the numbers in the size column will not be the same.)

For starters, let's try making a copy of MATH.BAS on the same diskette.

Making a Copy of a File on the Same Disk

The copy command is just what you'd expect it to be: **copy**. There cannot
be two files on the same disk with the same name, however, so if you want
a duplicate of MATH.BAS on this disk, you'll have to give the copy another
name. Type:

copy b:math.bas b:newmath.bas ENTER

One-Drive Systems
Substitute **a:** for **b:**.

Check the directory again to see NEWMATH.BAS listed. One-drive users
notice that the MS-DOS disk doesn't have to be in the drive to use the copy
command. It's an internal command, and it stays in memory even when the
MS-DOS disk is removed.

Copying a File to a Different Disk

Since the MS-DOS disk is not needed for file copying (once MS-DOS is "booted up"), it's a simple matter to copy files from one disk to another by simply specifying drives. The disk containing your files (which we'll refer to as the *source* disk) is already in Drive B, so two-drive users, put another blank, formatted disk (the *target* disk) in Drive A, and type:

copy b:math.bas a:math.bas [ENTER]

Notice it's perfectly all right to use the same name if copying to another disk.

To copy a file from Drive A to Drive B, just reverse the drive designations when you give the **copy** command.

Hard-Drive Systems

All you have to remember is that the hard drive is named Drive C. MS-DOS is on it, as well as all your files. To copy from the hard drive to a floppy, put the floppy in Drive A and use the command **copy c:math.bas a:math.bas** [ENTER]

One-Drive Systems

To copy a file from one disk to another in a single-drive system, it's necessary to fool the computer into thinking it has two drives. At the A⟩ prompt, type:

copy a:math.bas b:math.bas [ENTER]

The computer responds with:

```
Insert diskette for drive B: and
strike any key when ready
```

Remove the data disk from the single drive, and insert a second formatted disk. Strike any key. MS-DOS reports that it has copied one file and returns the A⟩ prompt. It still thinks of the diskette as Drive B however, so to see a directory of it, you must type:

dir b: [ENTER]

A simple **dir** command (without the drive designation) causes MS-DOS to ask you to insert the disk for Drive A. Put the *original* disk back in and strike any key, and you're back to a single drive, named A.

MS-DOS version 3.2 has an enhanced **copy** command, **xcopy**. Like the **copy** command, **xcopy** copies files from one disk to another. It can also copy directories and subdirectories from disk to disk and can make these copies between disks with different formats. To make full use of **xcopy** requires some understanding of advanced DOS features, so it's covered in Volume Two.

SUMMARY

* To copy a file to the same disk you must give the file a new name.
  Example: **copy b:oldname b:newname**
* To copy a file to a different disk, you may use the same name, but change the drive designation.
  Example: **copy a:oldname b:oldname**
* Files created in BASIC are automatically given the extension .BAS.

Shortcuts and Wildcards

Shortcuts

MS-DOS remembers which drive is the "current" drive. If MATH.BAS is in Drive A and you want to copy it, you don't have to specify A:MATH.BAS. The computer will automatically look on Drive A for any file it is asked for. If it doesn't find the file on A, it will say File not found.

To copy MATH.BAS from Drive A to Drive B, type:

copy math.bas b:math.bas [ENTER]

This reads, "Copy MATH.BAS (from Drive A, the default or current drive) to Drive B, and also call it MATH.BAS on Drive B."

The **copy** command can be further shortened by allowing MS-DOS to assume that the name of the copy will be the same as the name of the original. Typing:

copy math.bas b: [ENTER]

...means, "Copy MATH.BAS (from the default drive) to Drive B and give the copy the same name as the original."

Changing the Default Drive

The default drive is usually Drive A and normally that's where the MS-DOS system disk is kept. That's why the system prompt is A>. (In systems with a hard disk, the default is usually changed to Drive C.) Changing the default is simply a matter of typing:

b: [ENTER]

Now the system prompt is B>, and it won't be necessary to specify the **b:** drive designator when you ask for files from the disk in Drive B.

What Happens When MS-DOS Is Not in the Default Drive?

It's convenient to have the default be the drive which holds your data files (in this case, B), but what happens when you type an external MS-DOS command, like **diskcopy**, or **basic**? MS-DOS will now look at Drive B, but if the MS-DOS disk is in Drive A, those commands are still located down there. Typing an external command alone will result in an error message.

To tell MS-DOS to look for commands on Drive A when some other drive is the default, type:

path a: [ENTER]

The \ is on the [7] key in the numeric keypad. (On the 1200, the \ is located to the left of the *left* [Shift] key, and on the 3000s, it's up and to the left of the backspace [←] key.) Be sure the [NUM LOCK] light is not on.

Now, you can work in Drive B, but should you give a command that requires a file in Drive A, MS-DOS will be able to find it. The path a:\ search route will be remembered by the computer until it is turned off or rebooted, or until a new path is assigned.

Return the default to A by typing:

a: [ENTER]

One-Drive Systems

If any external MS-DOS commands need to be accessed, you will be prompted to `Insert Disk for Drive A:`. Simply swap disks and MS-DOS will, once again, pretend your disk drive is Drive A. After the command, you'll be asked to reinsert the diskette for Drive B.

Wildcards

The * character can be used as a *wildcard* to take the place of a file name or extension. * can be used to copy a whole group of files, all with the same name or extension. For example:

copy *.bas b: would copy all BASIC files from Drive A to Drive B, and give them the same names.

copy sample.* b: would copy all files named SAMPLE, no matter what extension each had, from Drive A to Drive B.

Let's try several examples. With the data disk containing your sample BASIC files in Drive B, type:

b: `ENTER`

...to change the default to Drive B, then:

copy *.bas *.dog `ENTER`

which means, "Copy all files with the extension **bas** to files with the *same* filename but with an extension **dog**."

Each BASIC file name appears on the screen as it is being copied. When the `B>` prompt returns, pull a directory. There will now be eight files on the disk--the original four with .BAS extensions and four duplicates with .DOG extensions. (Remember, in naming your files you can make up the three-character extensions as well.)

Try it again, this time using the extension .CAT.

copy *.dog *.cat [ENTER]

Now the directory shows twelve files. This "wildcard" feature can be useful for duplicating a series of matching "templates" or formats. For example, you might use Multiplan to design a spreadsheet called INCOME.MAY and another one called EXPENSE.MAY. Then, back in MS-DOS, copy all * .MAY files to *.JUN, then to *.JUL and so on.

Another approach would be to copy all EXPENSE.* files to some other file name. Try it with our GREETING files. Type:

copy greeting.* howdy.* [ENTER]

All three GREETINGs are duplicated to new files called HOWDY.

Wildcards with Directories

The wildcard can also be helpful when looking at directories. To see a list of only the BASIC files on default Drive B, type:

dir *.bas [ENTER]

In a large directory, when you're looking for something in particular, this is very helpful. Try it again using ***.dog** and again with ***.cat**.

Try it when the file name is known, but not the extension:

dir math.* [ENTER]

...or when only part of the file name is known:

dir greet* [ENTER]

This last one will be especially handy as your directories grow and will be a big help if you plan for it by naming related file names with the same few letters--for example: SALES1, SALES2, SALES3, etc. With a set of related files, a request for **dir sales*** will produce a directory of all files beginning with SALES.

Copying an Entire Disk Using the Wildcard

When the default is Drive A (A>), **copy *.* b:** copies *all* files from Drive A to Drive B. When the default is B, **copy *.* a:** copies *all* files from B to A.

Copying is a good way to clean up fragmented files. Remember when we discussed files being broken up to fit vacant sectors on the disk? A straight diskcopy will copy the sectors exactly as they are on the original disk. **copy *.***, on the other hand, will find all the parts of a file on the source disk and record them in a nice contiguous file on the target disk. Wildcard copying is a good reorganization tool to use when you suspect things are getting a bit scattered on the original disk.

Try it. With the default set to B>, and a formatted disk in Drive A, and the sample disk in Drive B, type:

copy *.* a: ENTER

One-Drive Systems
It will be necessary to fool the computer again. Since the Sample disk is in Drive A, type the command **copy *.* b:** ENTER. You'll be prompted to switch disks back and forth until the copying is complete.

By the way, *.* is usually pronounced "star dot star."

Deleting Files Using the Wildcard

When a particular project is finished and you want to clean up the disk, a whole series of similar files can be deleted using the wildcard and the **del** command. At the B> prompt, type:

del howdy.* ENTER

...and check the directory. All three HOWDYs are gone. Next type:

del *.dog [ENTER] to remove all the .DOG files. Leave the .CAT files for the next chapter.

Any individual file can be deleted with the **del** command by simply following the command with the file's full name.

Using the ? Wildcard

The ? is a special wildcard used to replace a *single letter*. If you were looking for a file named FRANCES2, and you couldn't remember if it was spelled FRANCES or FRANCIS, you could type: **dir franc?s2**. In this particular case, the * wildcard would have been less precise, because the * replaces everything that follows, whereas the ? only replaces a single letter. While **dir franc*** would have found FRANCES2 for you, it would also have found FRANCES3, FRANCES4, and so on.

Practice using the ? wildcard before moving to the next chapter, but don't delete any files at this time.

Type:

dir *.?A?

to display all files with an A in the middle of the extension.

SUMMARY

* MS-DOS remembers which is the default drive. If no drive designation is specified with a file name, MS-DOS looks on the default drive.
* To change the default drive from A to B, type **b:** [ENTER].
* In a copy operation, if no new file name is given, MS-DOS will give the new file the same name as the old.
* If the MS-DOS disk is in Drive A and the default has been changed to B, type **path a:** [ENTER] to make the computer search Drive A if it doesn't find what it's looking for on Drive B.
* The * wildcard takes the place of file names or extensions. It can also be used if only part of the filename is known. Example: GREET* for GREETING.

* The * wildcard can be substituted for *both* file names and extensions. To copy all files, use ***.***.
* The ? wildcard takes the place of an individual character. Example: FRANC?S for FRANCES or FRANCIS.

CHAPTER 20

Creating Files with COPY.COM

We've talked about how the **copy** command makes duplicate files, but there are several other things it can do. For example, it can be used to copy from the *console* to the disk. That means you can type a document on the keyboard, then save it to the disk as a file. No need to go into BASIC or your word processor or anything else. Just type and save. This is no substitute for a word processor, mind you, but it's good for creating a quick note, and we'll use it to create some more sample files.

Sample File 1 - NAMELIST

The **copy** command is used the same way we used it before; **copy** *source* to *destination*. The source in this case is the **con**sole because you'll be typing the text in at the keyboard. The destination is the drive, and the file name you want it saved under. With the MS-DOS disk in Drive A, a formatted disk in Drive B and the A⟩ prompt on the screen (return to it if you're not already there), try this one:

copy con b:namelist `ENTER`
Winston Churchill `ENTER`
William Shakespeare `ENTER`
Jacques Cousteau `ENTER`
Elizabeth Taylor `ENTER`
Saul Flintstein `ENTER`

116

To tell MS-DOS when you're finished with **copy con**, press [CTRL] [Z] (hold down the [CTRL] key and tap [Z]) or just press [F6]. This will appear at the bottom of your list:

^Z

Press [ENTER] again and NAMELIST is recorded on the data disk. Check the directory to verify.

Single Drive Systems
The **copy** command does not require the MS-DOS disk to be in place. Put the data disk in the drive, and don't specify a drive designation when typing the file name.

Sample File 2 · NOTE

Let's type a little note to go with the list of names. Call this one NOTE:

copy con b:note [ENTER]
Dear Barbara, [ENTER]
Here is the list of people I've invited to the party. [ENTER]
Hope they can all come. [ENTER]
[ENTER]
J.K. [ENTER]
[ENTER]
^Z [ENTER]

As you can see, the [ENTER] key is not there just to make things happen in MS-DOS; it also serves as the "carriage return" when typing more than one line. (If you're wondering about that extra [ENTER] between the signature and the ^Z, it's for something we have up our sleeve for a future chapter...)

Limitations

If you've used a word processor, you know that it does great things when it comes to editing and moving text around. A good word processor is to a typewriter approximately what a Maserati is to a pogo stick. **copy con**, when used to create text files, fits into that spectrum somewhere in the "moped" area. It gets you there, if you're not in a hurry, but no frills. If you make a mistake, the [BACKSPACE] or [←] key erases as the cursor backs up. MS-DOS does have a text editor called EDLIN, and we'll be looking at it in Chapter 26.

Displaying Files

You've used MS-DOS like a typewriter to create new files. To retrieve and look at them, use the **type** command. Check the directory to verify their exact names and to make sure they're actually there. Pick one you'd like to see and type:

type b:namelist [ENTER]

There's the list. Try the same thing with NOTE.

The **type** command is used primarily to view data files--those plain-English files created by you. To see what happens when you try to use **type** to read machine-language files, try it on FORMAT.COM on the MS-DOS disk.

BASIC language files, as well as data files created by other application programs, can generally be read with **type**. But they will contain some odd-looking characters and won't be formatted the way you'd see them if you had the application program up and running. **type** can be a "quick and easy" way to check a file to determine whether it is the one you're thinking of.

SUMMARY

* Type **copy con b:newfile** to create a file named NEWFILE from the keyboard and save it on the disk in Drive B.
* End the file with [CTRL] [Z] or [F6] (displays ^Z).
* **copy con** does not do wraparound or permit editing.
* Use EDLIN (Chapter 26) for advanced editing capabilities.
* Use **type b:newfile** to view a file named NEWFILE that is stored on the disk in Drive B.

CHAPTER 22

Printing Files

In Chapter 3, you learned how to print what is on the screen. There are several ways to print files from the *disk*. The first and simplest is the all-purpose **copy** command.

Copying from a Disk to the Printer

You learned in Chapter 20 how to copy from the console to disk. In similar fashion, you can copy from disk to printer, by simply specifying the file as the source and the printer (**prn**) as the target. Try it with PARTY. Again, be sure to have the disk containing your text files in the default drive, and the printer ON and ready. Type:

copy party prn ENTER

PARTY goes directly to the printer, without ever appearing on the screen.

Copying from the Console to the Printer

Since it's possible to copy from the console to disk and from disk to printer, why not copy from the console right to the printer? Type:

copy con prn ENTER

Now type something relevant:

"You are old, Father William," the young man said,
"And your hair has become very white;
And yet you incessantly stand on your head -
Do you think, at your age, it is right?"

^Z ENTER

The CTRL Z marks the end of the file. Pressing ENTER sends it to the printer.

Printing Files with the "Printing Queue"

When you need to print a number of files, and you don't want to wait for the printing to finish before you can use the computer, you can stack them up in a line, or "queue," to print automatically, while you do something else. It may appear that the computer is doing two things at once, but what is actually happening is called "time sharing." When you're not actually typing a character at the keyboard, the computer takes advantage of the pause, however brief, to go back to printing files.

Since there are only three text files on your disk so far, to make the demonstration a little more impressive, let's print each one twice. The command to print files into a print queue is simply **print**. As soon as you give the command, start typing something else--anything to demonstrate to yourself that the computer isn't "locked up" during the printing operation; that it will allow you to do other things with the computer while files are being fed to the printer. The impact of this feature will become quite dramatic when you have long files of your own to print later.

print note namelist party note namelist party

One-Drive Systems
print is an *external* command, which means that the MS-DOS disk is needed. Specify that the text files are on the imaginary Drive B. Put the MS-DOS disk in first and type:

print b:note b:namelist b:party b:note b:namelist b:party

You'll be prompted to insert the diskette for Drive B, which is your data disk. Once it's in, press any key and printing will begin. The diskette in Drive B cannot be removed until the printing is finished.

After pressing ENTER on the Tandy 1000s and 3000s, the **print** command will ask for the name of the "list device." Simply press ENTER to use the PRN, printer device.

Once printing begins, the message on the screen tells you that:

```
B:PARTY    ↓        is currently being printed
B:NAMELIST↓         is in queue
B:NOTE     ↓        is in queue
B:PARTY    ↓        is in queue
B:NAMELIST↓         is in queue
B:NOTE     ↓        is in queue
```

Notice that each file is printed on a separate sheet of paper. The ^Z, called the *end of file marker*, causes the printer to feed a new sheet so the files don't all run together.

Adding to the Print Queue

Up to ten files can be in the queue at any one time. In the event your list of files exceeds that number, you can add on to the end of the queue as printing of the first files is completed. Suppose, for example, you had fifteen files named ONE through FIFTEEN. Only files ONE through TEN could go into the queue to start with, but once the first five were printed, you could add in the five that wouldn't fit using the following form of the **print** command:

print eleven/p twelve thirteen fourteen fifteen

See the /**p** after the first file name? That's the signal to *add* these names to the queue. The /**p** affects the name immediately preceding it *and all names that follow*.

Removing (Canceling) Files from the Print Queue

If, in the above example, you started printing then changed your mind about files EIGHT, NINE, and TEN, give the cancel command:

print eight/c nine ten

Again, the **/c** goes after the first name in the cancellation list, and ahead of those that are to be removed from the queue.

Terminating the Print Queue

To terminate the printing and cancel the queue altogether, type:

print /t

SUMMARY

* To print a file named FILEONE from disk, type **copy fileone prn** [ENTER].
* To print directly from the keyboard, first type **copy con prn** [ENTER]. Then type your text. Press [CTRL] [Z] then [ENTER] to start printing.
* To print a number of files (named FILEONE, FILETWO, FILENEXT, etc.) in a printing queue, type **print fileone filetwo filenext**...etc. [ENTER].
* To add to the print queue, include **/p** following the first file name in the list of files to be added. Example: **print eleven/p twelve thirteen** ...etc. [ENTER].
* To remove (cancel) files from the print queue, include **/c** following the first file name in the list of files to be canceled. Example: **print eight/c nine ten** ...etc. [ENTER].
* To terminate the entire print queue, type **print /t** [ENTER].

CHAPTER 23

Renaming Files

When you create files with MS-DOS or an application program, you may assign them names on a more-or-less spur of the moment basis. If you use MS-DOS to keep files organized by watching the directories, deleting extraneous files, copying, combining and so on, you will also want to do some renaming. You may, for example, end up with a set of files named BUDGET, BUDGET.JUL, BGT.JUN, APRIL.BGT, MAYBGT.DAT, and some other variations as a result of forgetting, in one month, what you used in previous months. Or there may be several operators, each with a personal style of naming files.

At reorganizing time, the **rename** command allows you to change your mind about what a file is named without copying it to a new file and deleting the old one. The above examples could be changed, for instance, to BUDGET.APR, BUDGET.MAY, BUDGET.JUN and so on, so that they'd be orderly and all show up in a neat cluster on the directory. (More on this in Chapter 24). Let's try it on one of your sample files. At the B> prompt, type:

rename namelist names.txt [ENTER]

This changes NAMELIST to NAMES.TXT. The .TXT extension is a reminder to you that this is a text file, meaning that it is made up of words you can read. Some people label all their word processor and other text-type files this way. Files with the same name or extension, remember, can be manipulated as a group using the * wildcard. Use **rename** to add the .TXT extension to your other two text files:

rename party party.txt [ENTER]

...and try it using the wildcard as a shortcut:

rename note *.txt [ENTER]

Using the * means, "Rename NOTE to the *same name* plus .TXT."

Renaming a Group of Files Using the Wildcard

Check the Directory to see what has been changed. Now rename a whole group of files using the wildcard:

rename *.txt *.dat [ENTER]

This example changed all files with the extension .TXT to files with the extension .DAT. The file names themselves didn't change.

The wildcard can also take the place of the extension, of course. For example, if you had a group of files named BUDGET.MAY, BUDGET.JUN, BUDGET.JUL and so on, and wanted to change them to EXPENSES.MAY, EXPENSES.JUN etc., you would type:

rename budget.* expenses.* [ENTER]

SUMMARY

* To change the name of a file called OLDNAME to NEWNAME, type **rename oldname newname** [ENTER].
* The * wildcard can be substituted for either the old name or the new when only the extension is to be changed. Example: to change the extension on FILENAME.OLD to NEW, type **rename filename.old *.new** [ENTER].
* The * wildcard can also be substituted for the extension.

CHAPTER 24

Sorting Files

Putting a Directory in Alphabetical Order

The order in which file names appear in a directory depends upon how the files were saved in the first place. If you write and save them one at a time, the name of each new file will usually be added to the bottom of the directory. As files are deleted and others added, the names in the directory will end up in a seemingly random order. The names can, however, be put in alphabetical order with the **sort** command.

In order to sort files, MS-DOS temporarily stores information on the MS-DOS disk, so its write-protect tab must be removed, even though the directory you're going to sort is on Drive B. Be sure you are using a working copy of the MS-DOS diskette, and not the original!

Put the directory of your data diskette on the screen and look at it. See that the names of the files are not in any particular order. Now, with the A⟩ prompt on the screen, type:

dir b: ¦ sort ENTER

The vertical line between the drive designator and the **sort** command is called a *pipe*. It is located on the 4 key on the numeric keypad at the right side of the keyboard. To use it, the NUM LOCK key must be toggled off. If the NUM LOCK light is lit, press it again to shut it off. (On the 1200, the pipe is located to the left of the *left* Shift key, and on the 3000s, it's up and to the left of the backspace ← key.)

One-Drive Systems
Type the command just as above. You'll be prompted several times to switch back and forth between the disks.

The Pipe

The pipe connects commands. It "pipes" the output of one command into the input of another. In the above example, you gave the command to go to the disk and fetch the directory. Instead of outputting that directory right to the screen as usual, MS-DOS sent it to the *sort filter*, a little program that takes what it receives and puts it in alpha or numeric order. After this brief detour, the directory finally went to the screen.

The directory you just sorted does not stay sorted, however; that's not the intent of the **sort** command. It only *displays* the sorted output. Type **dir b:** and you'll see the directory in its regular, unsorted format. The output of a sort must be saved to a file if it is to be used later, without having to sort again.

Sending Output of the Sort Command to a File

The pipe (¦) sends the output of a command to another command. The *greater-than* symbol (>) sends the output to a file. Type:

dir b: ¦ sort > b:dirfile [ENTER]

This set of orders does the following:

1. calls up the directory of Drive B
2. and pipes it into the **sort** command
3. which arranges the directory in alphabetical order
4. then sends the sorted output to a file on Drive B named DIRFILE

Notice that since you sent the directory to a file, it didn't go to the screen. If DIRFILE had existed, it would have been written over. Since it didn't exist, MS-DOS simply created the file.

Type **type b:dirfile** ENTER to see the permanently sorted copy of the directory. Caution: this is just a text file; it is not automatically updated each time there is a change in the *actual* directory.

Sending Output of the Sort Command to the Printer

When the **sort** program finishes with the directory, it has to send it somewhere. If you don't specify, it automatically goes to the screen. Adding a file name after the > sends it to a file, and adding **prn** after the > sends it to the printer. Type:

dir b: ¦ **sort** > **prn** ENTER

This time, *you* explain what each part of the above command did.

Sorting on Other Columns

Sorting the way we have done it so far puts the output in alpha (or numeric) order, with sorting performed on the first letter of each line. The first letter of each line is called *column one*. The second letter in each line forms vertical column two, and so on. Suppose you wanted the output of this directory sorted in such a way that all the .BAS files were together and all the .TXT files were together. The simplest way would be to arrange the file names so their extensions are in alphabetical order.

Put the directory back up on the screen and count over to the beginning of the file name extensions. The longest name (GREETING) has the maximum of eight characters, and there is one space between those long names and their extensions, so all the extensions must begin in column ten, right? Count for yourself.

To sort by extension (column ten), type:

dir b: ¦ **sort** /+1Ø ENTER

To sort on file *size*, count over to the end of the extensions, plus one space, and you're in column 14. This is where the next area, file size, actually begins. Type:

dir b: ⦙ **sort** /+14 [ENTER]

Since column 14 contains numerical data, the sort is displayed in increasing numerical order.

Reverse Order Sorting with /r

Descending order, either alpha or numeric, requires only the addition of /r to the **sort** command. The /r goes in front of the column number. Type:

dir b: ⦙ **sort** /r/+14 [ENTER]

Try reverse sorting on column 1.

Sorting a File

We've been using the directory of Drive B as an example, but directories are not the only thing that can be sorted. The **sort** command can be extremely useful for organizing files which contain lists, providing the list is in column form or sorting is to be performed on only the first letter in each line. Examples:

Creating the file in strict column form requires the use of the [TAB] key. Two tabs after the shorter names and one tab after Elizabeth line up all last names in column 17.

Winston   Churchill
William   Shakespeare
Jacques   Cousteau
Elizabeth   Taylor
Saul   Flintstein

Here's another approach:

Churchill, Winston
Shakespeare, William
Cousteau, Jacques
Taylor, Elizabeth
Flintstein, Saul

This traditional arrangement sorts on the first letter of the last names in column 1. Let's try the second example. Open a new sample file called NEWLIST. Remember how?

copy con b:newlist [ENTER]

...and type the list, last name first, as above. Don't forget the **^Z** [ENTER] at the end.

Once the new file is created, sorting it requires this form of the **sort** command:

sort < b:newlist [ENTER]

Notice there is no pipe this time. The reason is that there is only one command: **sort**. We used the > to send *output* to a file a moment ago; this time we're using the < (less-than) to obtain *input* to the sort filter from the file named NEWLIST. NEWLIST appears on the screen with the last names in alphabetical order.

How about sorting a file and saving the result as a new file?

Saving the Contents of a Sorted File

If you think about this one, you can probably guess how to do it:

sort < b:newlist > b:lastname [ENTER]

We sorted using input from NEWLIST and sent the output to a new file called LASTNAME. Output went to the new file, not to the screen.

SUMMARY

* To sort a directory on Drive B, type **dir b:** ¦ **sort** [ENTER].
* The ¦ (pipe) is on the [4] key on the ten-key pad. [NUM LOCK] must be off. On the 1200, ¦ is to the left of the *left* [Shift] key, and on the 3000s, it's to the left of the backspace [←] key.
* To send output of the **sort** command to a file, add > and the file name to the end of the **sort** command.
* To send output of the **sort** command to a printer, add > and **prn** to the end of the **sort** command.

* To sort on a column other than the first, add /+ and the column number to the end of the **sort** command.
* To sort in reverse alpha or numeric order, add /r to the end of the **sort** command. If sorting on a column, add /+ and the column number *after* the /r. Example: **dir b:** ¦ **sort /r/+14** [ENTER].
* To sort the first column of a text file, type **sort** < and the file name [ENTER].
* To save the sorted contents of OLDLIST, a file in Drive B, in a new file (NEWLIST) on the same drive, type **sort** < **b:oldlist** > **b:newlist** [ENTER].

CHAPTER 25

Searching Files

Searching a Directory

In the last chapter, we organized the directory by putting it in alphabetical or numeric order. As your directories grow, even this may not be enough to allow you to find what you're looking for quickly. In Chapter 19, you searched through the directory for specific file names by simply typing **dir** and the name, or **dir** and a partial name, along with a wild card.

The **find** command will search for any *group* of characters. For example, you put on the disk several files that contained names. You can't remember anything about the file names except that they probably included the letters NAME. The files could be called MYNAME85, NEWNAME2, THE$NAME, or who knows what.

In order to search through a directory, you first give the **dir** command, then "pipe in" the **find** command--just as you did in the last chapter with **sort**. To find the *character string* NAME in the directory of Drive B, type:

dir b: ¦ **find "NAME"** (ENTER)

A couple of things to notice in this command: the string to be searched for must be in quotes, and capitalization must be exactly as it appears in the directory. We give most of our commands to MS-DOS in lowercase, even though it will accept both lower and uppercase. In the directory, however, MS-DOS converts all file names to uppercase, so to look for a file name, you have to use uppercase. The screen displays two file names containing NAME:

```
NAMES     DAT         75    10-03-87  12:34a
LASTNAME             95    10-04-87  10:15a
```

Your dates and times will, of course, be different.

Searching a Text File

The real benefit of the **find** command is in searching through text files. Searching a file does not require the pipe and does not require you to already be in the file. For example, with the B> prompt on the screen (A>, if you have only one drive), search through NEWLIST for the name Winston:

find "Winston" newlist [ENTER]

First you told it to *find*, then *what* to find, and finally *where* to find it. Notice that Winston has a capital W in the command because that's how it occurs in the file. If you're not sure if a word will be capitalized in the file, simply leave out the first letter altogether; in this case, search for "inston".

```
----------- newlist
Churchill, Winston
```

The entire line is displayed; not just the search string. That's why it's okay to leave out part of the word. Try this one:

find "Wi" newlist [ENTER]

This time it found two lines in the file that contained the requested string:

```
----------- newlist
Churchill, Winston
Shakespeare, William
```

Requesting the Line Number of the Searched-for String

Once MS-DOS has verified that the string does indeed exist in your file, what good does it do you? If you want to change something in the string, you have to open up the file and are then faced with the problem of finding the string all over again. Answer: The **find** command can tell you exactly what line the string is on. Then you can go into the file using the MS-DOS editor (*EDLIN*-- coming up in the next chapter) and make the repair.

Let's look for Elizabeth Taylor. Type:

find/n "liz" newlist [ENTER]

And the computer responds with:

```
----------- newlist
[4]Taylor, Elizabeth
```

find/n means, "Find it and give its line number." In the next chapter, we'll remember line 4 and do something with it.

Finding All Lines That *Do Not* Contain the String

Another extension to the **find** command makes it possible to find all words in the NEWLIST file that do *not* contain the string "Wi", type:

find/v "Wi" newlist [ENTER]

The /v causes the find filter to "filter out" the string, displaying all other lines.

```
----------- newlist
Cousteau, Jacques
Taylor, Elizabeth
Flintstein, Saul
```

Counting the Number of Times the String Occurs

The last **find** option available is /c. This extension doesn't display the string, it just counts the number of times it appears in the file and reports the count. Since these **find** features can be used with directories, let's search the directory of the MS-DOS disk for something we can find in a large enough quantity to be semi-impressive. How about the file name extension COM? Don't forget the pipe:

dir a: ¦ **find/c "COM"** [ENTER]

Because you changed the default drive to B⟩ for convenience in working with the data disk, it is necessary to specify the drive when asking for the directory of Drive A. As long as B is the default drive, MS-DOS automatically looks there, unless otherwise instructed.

Combining Two Find Features

There are three extensions to the **find** command: /n which gives line number, /v which displays all lines that do not contain the string and /c which just counts. The /v and /n features ("parameters") can be used together, but do not combine /c with either of them. Try this:

find/n /v "Wi" namelist [ENTER]

And here are the three entries that *don't* contain "Wi", complete with their line numbers:

```
------------ namelist
[3]Cousteau, Jacques
[4]Taylor, Elizabeth
[5]Flintstein, Saul
```

SUMMARY

* To search a directory in Drive A for the character string *files*, type **dir a:** ¦ **find "files"** [ENTER].
* To search for the string *Lastname* in the text file NAMELIST, type **find "Lastname" namelist** [ENTER].

* Capitalization must be identical to the string in the file. If uncertain about capitalization of first letter in a word, leave the first letter out.
* If uncertain of the spelling of a string, search for the known part of it.
* To obtain the line number in text file NAMELIST of the string *Lastname*, type **find/n "Lastname" namelist** [ENTER].
* To find all lines in the text file NAMELIST that do *not* contain the string *Lastname*, type **find/v "Lastname" namelist** [ENTER].
* To count the number of times the string *Lastname* occurs in the text file NAMELIST, type **find/c "Lastname" namelist** [ENTER].
* The **find** command can have both the /**n** and /**v** extensions at the same time. The /**c** extension cannot be combined with either of the other two.

CHAPTER 26

Edlin: The MS-DOS Text Editor

Edlin (for 'edit line') is a very useful "accessory" program included on the 2.11 Series MS-DOS disk or on the 3.2 Series Supplemental Programs disk. As mentioned earlier, the ultimate textmaking machine is a good word processor. We offered the opinion that the spectrum ran something like this:

* A good word processor (like SCRIPSIT) = exotic sportscar.
* The MS-DOS **copy con** command = motorized bicycle.
* A typewriter = pogo stick.

To carry this little exaggeration one step further, we would probably classify Edlin as a Volkswagen Beetle; simple, compact and all that many users will ever need, but short on luxuries. We won't attempt to provide a complete course in Edlin in this introductory book, but we'll give you a quick overview. Volume 2 covers Edlin in great detail.

Creating a New File with Edlin

The first order of business is loading the Edlin program and naming the file you want to create, or, if it already exists, to edit. Type:

edlin jack.ltr [ENTER]

Edlin responds with:

New file
*

138

Like BASIC, Edlin is a self-contained program and therefore uses its own prompt (the *). As long as you're in Edlin, you won't see the familiar A> or B> system prompts. The * reminds you that you're in Edlin where only Edlin commands will work. MS-DOS commands are not available.

The first Edlin command you'll need is the 'insert text' command which is simply the letter **i**.

*i [ENTER]

Edlin responds with:

        1:*

Every line in an Edlin file has a number. That number is for use on the screen only; it doesn't become part of the text and won't show up when the file is printed out. The prompt is at line number 1, so let's type some text:

1:***Dear Jack,** [ENTER]
2:***Sorry you couldn't make it to the party last night.** [ENTER]
3:***You missed Liz Taylor, Winston Churchill, Saul Flintstein,** [ENTER]
4:***and Jacques Cousteau.** [ENTER]
5:***Your Pal,** [ENTER]
6:***JK** [ENTER]
7:*[CTRL] [C]

[CTRL] [C] tells Edlin that you've reached the end of your message.

You must watch the screen when you're using Edlin, and press [ENTER] at the end of the last word you think you can get on each line. While it is possible to put up to 253 characters in each numbered "line," Edlin does not provide the *word-wrap* feature most word processors include. Edlin will take up to 80 characters on one line, then drop to the next, even if it's in the middle of a word.

Inserting Text into a Line

If you were observant, you noticed we left a name out of our list. William Shakespeare was on the party list, but was not mentioned in this note to Jack.

An unfortunate oversight, but easily remedied. To return to a line in the file, simply type its number and press ENTER. The logical place for Shakespeare's name is at the beginning of line 4. Type:

4 ENTER

Line 4 appears in its existing form, along with a second 4:* directly underneath, suggesting the opportunity to make some changes. You don't want to retype the whole line, however; you just want to insert a name. Press the INSERT key once (Ins on the 1200 and 3000s). Now type **William Shakespeare**, press the space bar, then the INSERT key again. What you just did was switch on the insert mode, type some new text and switch the insert mode off.

Now, what about the rest of the line? Hold down the → key and watch it magically appear before your eyes:

```
4:*William Shakespeare and Jacques Cousteau,
```

Press ENTER. Would you like to see an even quicker way? Press 4 ENTER again to open up line 4. Press the INSERT key and type:

Mr. and Mrs. (Leave a space after **Mrs.**)

Press INSERT again, then press the F3 key. Zip! There's the rest of the line. Press ENTER to complete the editing of line 4, and type **1l** (the number one and a lowercase letter l) and ENTER. This tells Edlin to start with line 1 and list (display) the entire file. It now reads:

```
1: Dear Jack,
2: Sorry you couldn't make it to the party last night,
3: You missed Liz Taylor, Winston Churchill, Saul Flintstein,
4: *Mr, and Mrs, William Shakespeare and Jacques Cousteau,
5: Your Pal,
6: JK
```

The * in front of the contents in Line 4 indicates that 4 was the last line edited. What you've actually been doing in editing this line is replacing the original line 4 with a new one. When you typed **4** and the original line appeared along with another 4:*, MS-DOS told you, "Anything you put on this new line 4 will replace the original. You can insert text with the [INSERT] key, accept what was there by tapping the [→] or [F3] keys, or delete text, but whatever form the line has when you finish and press [ENTER] is what will go into the file."

Deleting Text from a Line

On second thought, it does seem a bit ludicrous to suggest that Mr. and Mrs. Shakespeare were there (he wasn't even married, was he?). To delete everything up to a certain letter, use the [F4] key. In this case, you want to delete Mr. and Mrs., which is everything up to the W in William. Press [4] [ENTER] to put line 4 back up on the screen, then do this:

[F4] [SHIFT] [W] (Hold down [SHIFT] and press [W]) [F3] [ENTER]

The [F4] told Edlin to delete everything up to the specified character, which was a capital W (designated by pressing [SHIFT] [W]), and [F3] caused it to retype the rest of the existing line. [ENTER] finished the editing job. Typing **1l** [ENTER] displays the file in its latest form, without the Mr. and Mrs.

Changing Your Mind

To replace Pal with Friend, press [5] [ENTER], then the [→] key to move past the word Your and type **Friend**. Before pressing [ENTER], change your mind and decide to leave Pal as it was. To undo a change before you press [ENTER], use the [ESC] (Escape) key. Just press it once and the line will look like this:

5:*Your Friend,\

The backslash means this new version of the line was cancelled. Press [ENTER] and list the file with **1l** and see that Your Pal, is just as it was.

Printing an Edlin File

Printing an Edlin file is no more difficult than printing any other MS-DOS file. Be sure your printer is hooked up and turned on, then simply press the

PRINT key (Ctrl Prt Sc on the 1200 and 3000s) once to tell MS-DOS that you want it to print what follows. List the file with **1l**, and as each line appears on the screen, it will be printed.

Press PRINT (or Ctrl Prt Sc) to turn off printing.

Ending the Editing

There are two ways to finish up an editing job: Pressing Q ENTER at the * prompt quits editing but does *not* save any changes you made since the last time the file was saved on the disk. Try it. A message appears asking you if you're sure you want to do that. Press N ENTER.

Pressing E ENTER at the * prompt ends the editing, saves the file to the disk in its new form, and exits Edlin. Press E ENTER.

There is much more to Edlin waiting for you in Volume 2, but you now know how to open a file, make insertions and deletions to it, save it, print it and return to DOS. That's enough Edlin to let you use it, but not enough to make you dangerous.

SUMMARY

* To open Edlin and start a file named LETTER, type **edlin letter** ENTER.
* Edlin's prompt is *.
* To insert text, type **i** ENTER.
* To end a file created in Edlin, press CTRL C.
* To edit a line, just type its line number and ENTER.
* To insert within a line, use the arrow keys to move to the desired place, press the INSERT key once, type the new text and press INSERT again.
* To delete everything up to a certain character, type the line number to put the line on the screen, then press F4, the character, and ENTER.
* To display the rest of the line, after an insertion or deletion, press F3.
* To cancel a change before pressing ENTER, press ESC.
* To print an Edlin file, press PRINT, then list the file with **1l** ENTER.
* Pressing Q ENTER at the * prompt quits Edlin but does not save changes.
* Pressing E ENTER at the * prompt saves the changes and exits Edlin.

Review of Part Three

Part Three has been an introduction to the MS-DOS commands that are used to handle your files. Files created using MS-DOS or the MS-DOS editor (Edlin) as well as files created with BASIC and some other application software can be manipulated with these commands.

Commands

b: or **c:**, etc. changes the default drive.

BASIC

BASIC loads the BASIC programming language.

> **LIST** or ⌷F1⌷ displays a BASIC program.
> **RUN** or ⌷F2⌷ runs a BASIC program.
> **LOAD** or ⌷F3⌷ loads a BASIC program from disk into memory.
> **SAVE** or ⌷F4⌷ saves a BASIC program to disk.
> **NEW** clears the current BASIC program out of memory.
> **CLS** clears the screen.
> **SYSTEM** exits BASIC and returns to MS-DOS.

Path

path a: causes MS-DOS to search for programs and files on Drive A if it cannot locate the programs or files on the default drive.

Copy

copy a:oldfile a:newfile creates a duplicate file on the same disk in Drive A. Different file names must be used. (OLDFILE and NEWFILE are sample file names.)

copy a:somefile b:somefile creates a duplicate file on different disks. Drive designator must be included with at least one file name. The file names can be identical. (SOMEFILE is sample name.)

copy somefile b: is a short cut for creating a duplicate file with the same name on a different disk.

copy con b:somefile creates a file from the keyboard and saves it on the disk in Drive B. End the file with [CTRL] [Z] [ENTER].

copy 1stfile + 2ndfile 3rdfile combines 1STFILE with 2NDFILE to create 3RDFILE. 1STFILE and 2NDFILE remain separate and intact.

copy somefile prn sends the file SOMEFILE from the disk to the printer.

copy con prn sends output of keyboard directly to printer. Send the file to the printer with [CTRL] [Z] [ENTER].

Type

type somefile displays the file SOMEFILE on the screen from the disk.

Print (1STFILE, 2NDFILE, etc. are sample file names.)

print 1stfile 2ndfile 3rdfile...etc. puts a series of files into a *print queue*.

> **print 4thfile/p 5thfile 6thfile** adds files to the queue.
> **print 3rdfile/c 6thfile** cancels files from the print queue.
> **print /t** terminates the print queue.

Rename

rename oldfile newfile changes name of OLDFILE to NEWFILE.

Sort

dir a: ¦ **sort** sorts directory of Drive A.

> Adding > and a file name to the end of the command sends output of the sort to that file.
> Adding > and **prn** to the end of the command sends output of the sort to the printer.
> Adding /+ and a column number to the end of the command sorts on the column number specified rather than column one.
> Adding /**r** to the end of the command sorts in reverse alpha or numeric order.

sort < **b:somefile** sorts a text file in Drive B named SOMEFILE.

sort < **b:oldfile** > **b:newfile** sorts contents of OLDFILE and saves sorted text in NEWFILE on a disk in Drive B.

Find

dir a: ¦ **find "Fred"** searches for the word Fred in the directory of Drive A.

find "Fred" somefile searches for Fred in a text file named SOMEFILE.

find/n "Fred" somefile obtains the number of the line that contains Fred in SOMEFILE.

find/v "Fred" somefile finds all lines that do not contain Fred in the file SOMEFILE.

find/c "Fred" somefile counts the number of times Fred occurs in SOMEFILE.

find/n and **find/v** can be combined into **find/n /v**.

Edlin

edlin somefile loads Edlin and creates a new or opens an existing file named SOMEFILE.

i inserts text.

⎡CTRL⎤ ⎡C⎤ terminates an Edlin file.

⎡INSERT⎤ toggles insert mode on and off.

⎡F4⎤ **X** deletes everything up to the character X.

⎡F3⎤ after an insertion or deletion displays rest of line.

⎡ESC⎤ cancels a change in a line if pressed before ⎡ENTER⎤.

⎡PRINT⎤ **1l** (the number 1 and a lower case letter l) prints an Edlin file as it is displayed on the screen.

⎡Q⎤ ⎡ENTER⎤ at the * prompt quits Edlin but does not save changes.

⎡E⎤ ⎡ENTER⎤ at the * prompt saves the edited file to disk and exits Edlin.

CHAPTER 28

Some Final Words

Congratulations! You've come a long way. We introduced you to your Tandy MS-DOS computer, helped you get up and running and showed you some necessary commands plus a few tricks. You have learned everything that most operators need to successfully use MS-DOS on a day-to-day basis.

You can now take whatever direction you want. If you are satisfied at this level of understanding, fine. If you want (or need) a deeper understanding of MS-DOS, pick up Volume 2 of this series, **MS-DOS, Advanced Applications** (Radio Shack Cat. No. 25-1507). It goes into great detail, explaining the advanced features, and showing how to use them to customize MS-DOS for your particular needs. To get the most from your Tandy system, now or later, it is worth obtaining a copy.

APPENDIX A
Tandy 3000 Series System Setup

Getting Started

Because of their advanced features, the Tandy 3000 Series computers need some preparation before they're ready to use. This is typically done by a Radio Shack technician as part of the purchase agreement.

If it has not been done, an error message appears when the computer is first turned on. This means you need to run the SETUP program.

Locate the Hard Disk Utilities diskette which came in the box with the computer. Place this diskette in the computer's floppy disk drive (the top drive if there are two) with the Tandy label facing up and toward you. Close the disk drive latch and press the key marked F1.

The SETUP Program

SETUP sets the internal clock, lets the computer know how much memory, how many and what kinds of disk drives are installed, and what type of monitor is being used. This information is stored in special memory inside the computer for recall each time the computer is turned on. Follow the instructions on the screen, answering Y or N to the questions. If, in the future, you want to change your responses to the SETUP program questions, simply insert the UTILITIES diskette into Drive A, and type **setup** at the A> prompt.

The Internal Clock

One of the SETUP program's duties is to set the computer's internal clock. This clock is run by an internal battery and provides MS-DOS with the accurate time and date.

The time stored by the internal clock and the time MS-DOS keeps track of can be different. It is possible to set MS-DOS (via the **time** and **date** commands discussed in Chapter One) to a different date and time than the internal clock. When the computer is reset or turned off then on, the MS-DOS time returns to the internal clock's time.

Hardware Configuration

Once the time and date are correct, SETUP displays the current hardware settings. To enter the correct options for your computer, press [N] [ENTER] in response to the prompt.

Study each configuration screen as it is displayed. If the settings are correct, press [Y] [ENTER]. If they are not, press [N] [ENTER], and follow the instructions to make the necessary changes.

The Installation and Operations Manual that came with your computer explains what information you will need and how to determine the correct settings for your particular configuration.

After the SETUP program has been run successfully, resume reading at Chapter One.

NOTE: If you have any hesitation about running the SETUP program or additional questions regarding what it does, contact your local Radio Shack dealer for assistance.

Index

Other Books by David A. Lien

MS-DOS, Volume 2, Advanced Applications,   Cat. No. 25-1507
ISBN 0-932760-42-2 $14.95

Learning BASIC for Tandy Computers, 2nd Ed.   Cat. No. 25-1500
ISBN 0-932760-43-0 $19.95

The TRS-80 Model 100 Portable Computer   Cat. No. 26-3819A
ISBN 0-932760-17-1 $14.95

The Tandy 200 Portable Computer   Cat. No. 26-3869
ISBN 0-932760-30-9 $19.95

Available from your Tandy/Radio Shack dealer.